FREE ACTION

STUDIES IN
PHILOSOPHICAL PSYCHOLOGY

Edited by
R. F. HOLLAND

FREE ACTION

by

A. I. MELDEN

LONDON

ROUTLEDGE & KEGAN PAUL

NEW YORK: HUMANITIES PRESS

First published 1961
by Routledge & Kegan Paul Limited
Broadway House, 68–74 Carter Lane
London, E.C.4

Printed in Great Britain
by Hazell Watson & Viney Ltd
Aylesbury and Slough

CONTENTS

v

PREFACE

THOSE who look for a definitive and simple elucidation of the concept of free action will not find it
in this work. This is only a preliminary inquiry in
which crucially important issues, that go unobserved
and unexamined in the familiar arguments pro and
con the possibility of free action, are brought to light
and examined in some detail. I hope I have succeeded
in exposing some of the obscurities and confusions in
which such arguments have been fatally enmeshed,
and in indicating some of the important features of
the concept of free action that need further explora-
tion. The argument in this book may well seem tortu-
ously detailed, but I know no other way of dealing
with the questions that arise. One topic seems to lead
on inexorably to another, until in the end it seems that
no single question can be raised without implicating
every other that bears upon the vast and complex
scene of human action. This I believe is a good sign.
Yet one must make a start somewhere and try as best
one can to do one thing at a time, leaving for sub-
sequent examination the many problems, complex
and difficult, that remain to be looked into but which
can only be touched upon briefly and at best schemati-
cally in a work of this limited size. To this end I begin
my positive argument by examining what might
appear to be all too simple matters, too simple indeed
to be worth any attention. Yet they are, as I try to
show, of absolutely central importance for any per-

spicuous grasp of the concept of a free action. The individual chapters of this book mark different phases of a developing argument and for the most part they cannot be treated as independent essays. If the reader is inclined to be impatient because I do not at once launch into a high-level discussion of free will, I can only ask him to be patient and to follow the argument, tortuous and even remote as it may sometimes appear to be, in the hope that its importance may become evident as it moves along.

I acknowledge gratefully the assistance I have received from the following persons: Mr. R. F. Holland, for his editorial assistance; my students, with whom I discussed many topics dealt with here, especially Dr. Charles Chihara who has read and criticized the whole of the manuscript; Professors Fred Hagen, Herbert Morris and Alexander Sesonske, who have given me the benefit of their criticisms of my discussion of desires; and most important of all, Professor Arthur E. Murphy for his encouragement, for the invaluable stimulus of many discussions I have had with him on these and related topics over a period of years, and for the benefit of the very useful criticisms of the manuscript as a whole which he has given me. Thanks also are due to the Research Committee For the Graduate School of the University of Washington, which provided funds for the typing of the MS.

A slightly altered version of Chapter V appeared in the October, 1960 issue of *The Philosophical Review*.

A. I. M.

INTRODUCTION

THAT a science of human conduct is possible, that what any man may do even in moments of the most sober and careful reflection can be understood and explained, has seemed to many a philosopher to cast doubt upon our common view that any human action can ever be said truly to be free. The rosy Baconian promises of the benefits to be derived from a knowledge of nature have appeared to be hollow to many a thinker viewing the possible extension of the methods of natural science to the sphere of human conduct. It is a bit of irony that even as the seventeenth-century investigators of nature were exercising their newly won freedom as they laid the foundations of modern science, some philosophers of the new science came to view with suspicion the common-sense conviction that human beings are free and responsible, just as soon as they turned their attention to man himself and sought to lay out the ground plan of psychology. It is, of course, a familiar view that Hume once and for all time laid to rest the growing disquiets of this sort in his polemic on the subject of causation and necessity and in his apparently innocuous suggestion that free action is to be distinguished from action that is not free, not by the absence of causal conditions but by the presence of certain specific sorts of mental causes. But these reassurances have not sufficed to allay the fears of all of his self-styled tough-minded followers. Not only have the consequences drawn from such a determinism produced dissension with respect to the possibility of freedom even in the ranks of modern-day Humeans, but more and more, and on grounds quite independent of the desire to do justice to our common belief that some conduct is free, even the appropriateness to mental phenomena of the deterministic model envisaged by Hobbes, Hume and others who have followed in their wake, has come under suspicion. For what has recently become evident is that a veritable maze of muddles pervade and surround the familiar accounts offered by classical determinists of just such central and crucial notions as those of action, consequence, motives, circumstances and conditions, intention, reason and the like. Indeed, the polemic between determinists and indeterminists all too frequently is conducted by both parties with an air of self-satisfaction concerning our understanding of the important logical features of these concepts. And if there is any ground for the recent suspicions that these, among other relevant concepts, need re-examination and a more careful scrutiny than they have received in the familiar debates between determinists and indeterminists, this surely is a matter of the very first importance not only in respect of the age-old problem of the so-called 'freedom of the will' but also in its bearing upon the legitimacy and the relevance to human action of a good deal of what passes for the science of psychology. Indeed, these matters will bear in important ways on any branch of philosophy which deals with human affairs, particularly on moral and social philosophy.

CHAPTER ONE

THE CASE AGAINST FREE ACTION

LET me begin by considering the following imaginable case. While visiting a friend late one afternoon I am offered whiskey. I know that if I drink on an empty stomach I shall feel the effects in such a way that I shall be careless when I drive home, that my reflexes will be seriously impaired and that the chances of my being involved in an accident on the crowded streets will be increased very sharply. Nevertheless, and despite my recognition of these facts, I decide to risk it. I imbibe, drive my car, and because my driving skill has been impaired, I hit and kill a pedestrian on my way home.

Ordinarily no one would hesitate to judge me morally and legally accountable. I knew, as I do now, the difference between right and wrong. I knew full well that what did in fact happen was just the sort of thing that might well take place under the circumstances; yet I chose to risk not only my well-being and life, but even that of another human being. No one compelled me to take drink by forcing it down my throat. No one compelled me to drive my car even after I had become somewhat tipsy, for even at that point I was aware that it would be safer to leave my car with my friend and return home by taxi. I knew what I was doing when I accepted the drink and did so freely, without constraint or compulsion of any sort. Clearly, then, I am responsible for what I did in running into and killing the pedestrian.

Yet these reflections on my responsibility can be and indeed have been challenged on familiar philosophical grounds. The challenge may take very many different forms, but I want to concentrate on a few familiar counter-arguments.

No man can be accountable for anything he does unless what he does is free, and no man's action is free unless he could have done otherwise. But I could not have avoided killing the pedestrian even though, had I been sober, I would not have hit him. For in point of fact I was tipsy and, given my state and the circumstances at the time of the accident, what did in fact happen, had to happen. For my tipsiness caused me, given the circumstances then present, to move the wheel, press the accelerator, and so on in precisely the way I did. Hence the event that consisted in the killing of the pedestrian was necessary, just as much so as any natural occurrence, *e.g.* the breaking of an egg when it rolls off the kitchen table and hits the floor. Could I have avoided being tipsy? Only if I could have refused the drink my friend proffered me. To be sure, if I had refused I would not have become tipsy, but equally if I had been in Timbuctoo I would not have been driving my car and I would not have been involved in the tragic accident. But it was no more possible for me to refuse the drink than for me to be in Timbuctoo. Given the relevant antecedent conditions, I had to be in my friend's house, and given the relevant psychological conditions and the circumstances then present, I had to accept the drink. For I am by nature easily tempted, venturesome, willing to take all sorts of risks even when I am fully aware of the fact that the odds are against me; and anyone knowing my character would have been able to predict unerringly that in these circumstances I would drink myself into a well-marked state of inebriation. Hence I could not possibly have done otherwise; I had to accept the drink my friend invited me to take. Nor was his conduct free or culpable in any way, since these observations about myself are paralleled by similar observations that can be made about him.

But is it not true that the condition of my character is after all the result of my own past doings, due, as Aristotle held, to prior exercises of choice? And if such exercises of choice occurred, then is it not true that at least *in cause*, as this is sometimes put, by choosing to do those things which would have resulted in the formation of a more cautious character than the one I actually had when I visited my friend, I could have refused the drink my friend offered me? Hence even if I could not have refused the drink, given the character I actually had, is it not true that I could have had a different character and hence, derivatively at least, that I could have acted in a different way?

But apart from the excessive intellectualization involved in this account of the formation of character—for after all such exercises of choice, in order to preserve the appearance of freedom, must be supposed to have taken place before my character exhibited any trace of the spoilage so markedly evident at the present time, and hence must have occurred at an age, surely not much later than infancy, in which rational choice

cannot be supposed plausibly to have taken place—
this riposte must surely fail. Not only choice, but all
of the other psychological factors that issue in action
are themselves enmeshed in the bonds of causal necessity: my perceptions, desires, interests, motives, needs,
no less than the character traits I now have or had at
any other time in the past. My past choices, like my
present character, had to be what they were; for given
their causally antecedent conditions they could not
have been other than what in point of fact they were.
To be sure, if such antecedent causal factors had
been other than what they were, I would not have
chosen as I had and developed the character I now
have. So too, if I had not been born and raised in the
circumstances in which I was in fact born and raised,
I would have been different from what I became. But
in this sense even a stone is free when it falls to the
ground, for one can say here too that if the conditions
had been different from what they were it would not
have fallen, but remained as it was, or in any other
state you will, given suitable causal antecedents. For
we can always specify contrary to fact conditionals
about human behaviour: I would not have hit the
pedestrian if I had not been driving my car, I would
not have been driving my car if I had returned home
by taxi, and so on. And if the import of the statement
that I could have avoided hitting the pedestrian is to
be given by means of such contrary to fact conditionals,
then it is vacuously true that I could have done otherwise than what in fact on any given occasion I did.
But whatever does happen, happens necessarily as it
does, for given the conditions of its occurrence, the
happening is causally necessary. Trace the causal

4

antecedents of my conduct and my character back into the past as far as one pleases, to the conditions of my birth and my training, what happens now when I act as I do must happen in precisely the way in which it does. Hence I am no more responsible for what I am and do today than I am for the causal conditions of my birth, the training I received and the character I have, than I am for the fact that my father married my mother.

It is then a hollow reassurance that Hobbes gives us when he declares that 'liberty and necessity are consistent . . . in the Actions which men voluntarily doe: which, because they proceed from their will, proceed from *liberty*; and yet, because every act of mans will, and every desire, and inclination proceedeth from some cause, and that from another cause, in a continuall chaine, (whose first link is in the hand of God the first of all causes,) they proceed from *necessity*'. (*Leviathan*, Pt. 2, Ch. 21.) If this be the liberty of men, it is not that of God, for his actions are not inextricably tangled, as those of men are, in a causal network of which the antecedents are motives, desires, etc. He chooses freely in a sense quite different from that applicable to men. To say that man acts freely is, according to Hobbes, to say that his action 'proceeds from his will', *i.e.* that his action has his will, namely, 'the last Appetite in Deliberating', as causal antecedent. (*Ibid.*, Pt. 1, Ch. 6.) But deliberation and appetite are for Hobbes causally necessary consequences of anterior happenings, as necessary as the flow of water through its channel. (*Ibid.*, Pt. 2, Ch. 21.) Hence, man could no more choose, will and act differently from the way he does, than water can move otherwise than the

5

way it does, and if this mode of speech is to be preserved for the conduct of man on the ground that his action would have been otherwise had its causal conditions been otherwise, why not for the flow of water through its channel? But if the distinction between natural occurrences and the human occurrences we commonly label 'free actions' is to be maintained simply on the ground that in the latter case, unlike the former, the peculiarly human occurrence of volition occurs as antecedent causal condition, this surely is a bit of verbal legislation that does not affect the substance of the matter. On this showing no distinction, *à propos* of the question of freedom, can be drawn between the conduct of a normal responsible agent and that of many a compulsively neurotic person; for if the former's conduct is to be labelled 'free' on the ground that, had the volition been otherwise the action would have been different, then in this vacuous and counterfeit sense, the neurotic is no less 'free' than the sane, and the worst moral derelict of a human being, whilst in that sorry condition, is capable of the greatest and most consistent moral heroism.

Worse follows if, in the manner viewed by Hobbes and many a recent follower, we look to bodily conditions and events for the 'genuine' causally operative conditions of human behaviour. For, to return to our imaginary case of the killing of the pedestrian, the impact that caused his death resulted from the depression of the accelerator, this in turn from the stimulation of the muscles of the leg, the stimulation occurred because of the abnormal state of certain portions of the central nervous system together with the stimuli received from the several senses when in my somewhat alcoholic manner I drove erratically down the road. Could I then have avoided hitting the pedestrian? Could I have avoided accepting the drink that led to the impairment of my bodily condition? But is it too fantastic to suppose that there are physiological states and occurrences characteristic of and peculiar to any phase of the whole background of the accident including those that transpired as I considered and accepted the drink? It would be *a priorism* at its worst to deny that there are characteristic physiological correlates of character traits, reflection, deliberation, choice, and so on. And now it begins to appear as if a complete causal explanation of the killing of our pedestrian can be given in terms of brain states, stimuli, muscle movements, the depression of the accelerator of the car, the latter's motion and resulting impact that affected the vital organs and thus caused the death of our unfortunate. In this account where is there room in which persons and their volitions, reflections, desires, etc., can operate? These are as much out of place in a complete physiological explanation of my condition and behaviour as they are in a complete account that can be offered of the motion of my car and the effect upon the pedestrian's life of the dreadful impact of the car upon his body. I said 'worse follows', for here there is no room for personal agency, there is nothing in this account that is 'my doing'—I am a helpless victim of the conditions in my body and its immediate physical environment.

But let the causal explanation of my behaviour be given in terms of my volitions, desires, interests, etc. (to what avail is it to mix these with physiological occurrences and states?), and equally well it seems to follow that I am a victim of all that transpires within and without me! For what I willed both when I accepted the drink proffered by my friend and when I drove my car turns out on this picture of what transpired, not something *I* really willed and did, but something that was made to happen by antecedent conditions, my mental condition, my inclinations, my desires, motives, and so on. If *these* are the causal factors and if these are subject to causal explanation in terms of antecedent psychological factors, then whatever happens is none of my doing but of these very psychological factors, themselves. Surely I am not any one of these factors, nor all of them; they may be 'mine' in some proprietary sense, but they, not I, do what they do since they, not I, are the psychological levers and pulleys that issue in whatever it is that does get done in the form of overt behaviour. It is, then, a vulgar mode of speech fostered by superstition or some incredibly obscure notion of personal agency that leads people to say that a *person* does anything at all; for in strict philosophic truth the actions with which we are commonly concerned are things that happen, goings-on that proceed from other goings-on in and about one. Just as it would be a mistake to attribute agency to the car and to blame it for the death of the pedestrian, so it would be a mistake to suppose that a person does anything and to blame him for it, when in ordinary speech we say he thinks, feels, wills, acts. These latter occurrences are the things that do whatever it is that does get done. There may be an obscure sense in which the motives, desires, volitions, etc., that issued in the overt behaviour of drinking and driving and the destruction of the life of our pedestrian are 'mine', but these are not strictly speaking *my* doing, since each of these can be explained not by reference to my *self*, but to other doings of like sort, the various events in the psychological mechanism. Hence it is that these causal factors are happenings in, or to, me, rather than things that I do; they are, simply, things that get done by means of prior happenings of like sort. And each of us, myself included, as I survey the natural history of our imaginary incident, is a victim, witting or not, of these goings-on that make *all* the difference to what, in our common and confused or downright mistaken way, we describe as the things that people do.

One omnibus rebuttal can, of course, be used at this point. If these considerations demonstrate the helplessness of persons in the face of all that mistakenly we describe as the things they do, they demonstrate equally well the helplessness of individuals with respect to what they allegedly think. For thoughts too are caused, and as such what I or anyone else thinks is a necessary product of all of the factors that determine our thoughts and beliefs. So one could argue equally well that it is not we who think and that what is thought is a matter with respect to which each of us is utterly helpless. It is futile to recommend or endorse any thoughts that might occur in us, for or against the doctrine that any of us is free. In each of us the thoughts are what they must be and all discourse, including the preceding argument, must on that view degenerate into purely natural phenomena wholly exempt in principle from rational appraisal.

Such a *tu quoque* unfortunately not only cuts both ways, it also leaves unimpaired the persuasive power of the arguments directed against our common-sense view that free action is possible. These arguments may not secure genuine conviction, yet they are troublesome. Of course something has gone wrong during the course of these arguments and the mistakes need to be brought into full view. The force of any philosophic paradox, as Hume once observed, can be dissipated through inattention alone, no less than by the persuasive techniques of counter-arguments. But unless attention is paid to the crucial notions employed in a philosophical argument and some measure of success attained in the effort to gain an understanding of them, these disturbing puzzles and paradoxes must return upon us with undiminished force whenever we reflect upon the considerations that prompt them. And philosophy is nothing if it is not inquiry and reflection; and it is unsuccessful if it does not provide us with that understanding of crucial concepts which alone can function as a relevant and effective counter-measure.

In the remainder of this essay I propose to examine in detail a number of questions that bear upon the paradox, not for the purpose of setting one counter-argument against another but in order to expose the misunderstanding of basic concepts that runs through the arguments presented above, with a view to helping to bring some of the basic logical features of these concepts into clearer focus.

CHAPTER TWO

CHARACTER AS CAUSAL CIRCUMSTANCE

CONSIDER the form of question, 'What made A do X?' We can imagine all sorts of situations in which this form of sentence would be employed; but is it clear from the form of the sentence employed what kind of explanation is appropriate? Consider the following:

(*a*) What made me take such a risk as to drive my car when I was tipsy? Answer: My foolhardiness.

(*b*) What made me drive the car so erratically? Answer: My tipsiness.

(*c*) What made me swerve the car? Answer: The sight of the dog lying in the middle of the road.

(*d*) What made me shiver? Answer: My fever.

(*e*) What made me wave my arm at the passers-by? Answer: I just felt like doing so.

Instead of the locution 'made me', other locutions involving 'cause' (what caused me to . . .?), 'reason' (what was the reason for my . . .?), 'why' (why did I . . .?), etc., might do just as well. And these same locutions are commonly employed *à propos* of natural objects (what made the motor sputter? what caused the motor to sputter? what was the reason for the sputtering of the motor? why did the motor sputter?).

It is natural, therefore, to suppose that throughout, the same general type of explanation is being called for (the differences between the various cases consisting only of differences in subject-matter), and hence that, just as in the case of the car, so in the case of myself the answers given specify standard and clear-cut cases of causal conditions.

Let us begin with a consideration of case (a). It is of course a familiar view that if one characterizes a person as foolhardy and thereby explains his foolhardy conduct, one is subsuming that conduct under a law-like hypothetical or series of such to the general effect that whenever circumstances in which he is placed are of the appropriate sort, he will take unreasonable risks, etc. But on the face of it, this view is open to the objection that persons can and on occasion do act out of character. Hence if my reply to the question, 'What made you do that?' is 'I am foolhardy, I suppose', it is implausible on the very face of it to suppose that I am offering a causal account of my action by subsuming it under a law-like hypothetical. 'I acted with caution', if true, does not establish that I am characteristically cautious; but neither does it falsify 'I am of a foolhardy character'. The action may not be the action of a cautious person even though, because it is correctly describable as cautious, it is the action that a cautious person might well be expected to perform.

But why should one expect a foolhardy person to act incautiously—if not recklessly, then let us say with a recognition of but a contempt for the large risks involved—unless the statement that he is foolhardy is at least a general statement about conduct? So it might be thought that the reason for retaining the description of a person as foolhardy even when in a given instance he is acting with commendable caution is due to the fact that our statement of the law-like hypothetical (which we gave above in a very schematic form) is somehow elliptical. In general, after all, foolhardy people act in a foolhardy manner, but when they do not, there are interfering causal conditions. Thus, we do not deny that salt is soluble (*i.e.* that when salt is put in water, it dissolves) when a specimen of salt fails to dissolve; the conditions have to be 'right', the water must be in a 'standard' condition. And why not therefore this same thing in the case of 'He is foolhardy'?

Now there may well be an ellipsis in the chemist's statement that salt, when put in water, dissolves (although there need not be an ellipsis at all if the statement is not one about causal laws or relations but only a common-sense generalization drawn from ordinary experience), but what is the ellipsis involved in the statement that persons, supposing them to be foolhardy, will act in appropriate circumstances in the expected way? In order to preserve the parallel with the chemist's statement about salt, we must suppose it to be understood that the conditions are normal. And how shall we define 'normal conditions'? Surely not as conditions which prevail in general; for in that case our statement ceases to be a law-like statement and reduces to the common-place that foolhardy people generally act in foolhardy ways. And unless these normal conditions can be defined, *i.e.* specified, the parallel with the chemist's statement breaks down completely. Someone might retort that after all there must be circumstances special to the case in which a foolhardy person acts out of character and behaves in this unexpected case with caution. No doubt; but even supposing that these circumstances are causal conditions, what is at issue is not the possibility of explaining the exceptional case, but what is meant by the description given of a person as foolhardy and whether in offering such a description in explanation of his conduct, what we are offering is a law-like hypothetical about his behaviour. One can preserve the appearance of a law-like statement by supposing that when we describe a person as foolhardy what we are saying is that unless there are interfering circumstances, such a person when placed in circumstances of a certain sort will act in such-and-such a manner. So stated our law-like statement may not be falsified by the exceptional case in which a foolhardy person acts out of character, but only because, 'interfering circumstances' being intolerably vague, our statement becomes impossibly useless and trivial. In any case, what is at issue is not whether there may or may not be conditions present in any given case that lead a person to act in or out of character, but whether any reference to these conditions is logically involved in our characterization of him as foolhardy. And that no such logical involvement holds is abundantly clear from the fact that I may well understand what it means to say that a person is foolhardy even though I may be totally in the dark as to why it is that in this, rather than that, case the foolhardy person acts in character. If this is so, we must abandon the attempt to reduce our categorical statement, 'I am foolhardy', to a hypothetical law-like statement, and with it the view that when I explain my conduct by confessing to being a foolhardy person I am simply subsuming that conduct under a general causal law.

Granted, however, that 'I am foolhardy' is a categorical statement that describes one facet of my character, does it not explain my conduct by specifying a condition in which, given certain specific causal factors, *i.e.* certain psychological occurrences, my foolhardy behaviour will issue as effect? Consider a metal rod in the state at, or very close to, absolute zero. Such a rod conducts electricity with little or no resistance; but it does this only if some occurrence takes place, say, the introduction of an electric current at one end of the rod. Yet its condition at absolute zero is a relevant causal condition of the observed effect of the virtually resistanceless flow of current. Now a person whose state of character may be described as foolhardy reacts rashly to various occurrences, but only if certain other causal conditions, namely, psychological events, take place. On occasion, however, such a person will not behave rashly, but then only because some one or more of these psychological conditions are absent. Hence even if statements about my character which I may make in explanation of my in-character behaviour are not themselves lawlike conditionals, such statements would seem to appear to cite relevant causal conditions—'state-conditions' if you like. 'This is the way I am—foolhardy—and under normal conditions, given the appropriate conditions, my expected behaviour follows causally.' For this reason, so the present argument runs, we can assert hypothetical statements about a person's conduct given the knowledge of his character. For if circumstances are appropriate, then given the occasions of action, a person who is foolhardy will behave in characteristically foolhardy ways.

Instead of examining more closely the status of our assertions about the character of persons, it may be well to turn our attention to the other end of the alleged causal chain. For whatever it is that being foolhardy consists in, what is of central interest in our inquiry is the alleged necessity of the given action under the appropriate causal conditions. And here it is of crucial importance that we ask, in connection with the argument presented above: Just what is the action that follows causally?

Before turning to this question, an important word of caution. The term 'cause' is one of the snare words in the philosophical lexicon. Failure to attend to the variety of ways in which it is employed is one of the sources of the confusions that surround the traditional controversy over the freedom of the will. For the present I am concerned with 'cause' either in the Humean sense of this term or, if this is alleged to be inadequate in certain respects, to the use of the term in scientific explanations of, say, physical or physiological events, in that sense of the term in which it is in fact employed in physics or physiology. Whether or not Hume's account of causation is adequate to these applications of the term 'cause' is a further matter not germane to my argument. What I shall be concerned to deny in the argument that follows is that the term 'cause' *when employed in these sciences* is applicable to those matters which, familiarly and on a common-sense level we cite in order to explain action: the motives, desires, choices, decisions, etc., of human beings. I do not, of course, deny that there are appropriate senses of 'cause' which can be intelligibly employed in these cases—these indeed I insist upon in the concluding chapter.

CHAPTER THREE

ACTION AND HAPPENING—
PROBLEMS AND PERPLEXITIES

WHEN a person drives his car, cautiously or not, certain very complicated series of actions take place. He starts the motor, manipulates the clutch, accelerates, turns, brakes the car, and so on. 'Driving one's car' is a very general description of what a person does that may apply to recognizably different series of actions; indeed, it is unlikely that a person who drives his car on different occasions performs precisely the same actions in the same order. To simplify matters let us consider just one action, say, signalling a turn, and to further narrow the scope of our inquiry let us suppose that this is done by raising one's arm as one sits at the wheel. Suppose then that at precisely 2.56 p.m. of a certain day someone signals a turn, what precisely is the happening for which a causal explanation in terms of character and other factors is to be given? Several things need to be sorted out and considered.

(1) Of course, one happening is the signalling. 'At precisely 2.56 p.m. A signalled' describes an event, a happening. A signalled—this is how he proceeded to make a turn.

(2) Whenever a person signals, he does something describable, not as signalling, but in some other way. 'How does one signal?' is an intelligible question and the appropriate answer would be 'By raising one's arm in such-and-such a way.' So one signals, by raising one's arm; stops the car by applying the brakes; starts the motor by turning the key in the ignition lock; and so on. In all of these cases one does X only by doing Y, where 'X' and 'Y' are distinct, not synonymous, descriptive expressions. So at 2.56 p.m. what happened, when the person signalled, is that he raised his arm—this is how he signalled.

(3) Whenever a person raises his arm certain muscles contract and certain other muscles relax in such a way that the arm structure is elevated. So at 2.56 p.m. certain muscle movements took place— this is how the arm gets raised.

It is unnecessary at this point to inquire further into still other events that must have occurred given the proceedings described in (3). Of course muscles must have been stimulated by nerve impulses transmitted from the central nervous system in the manner described by physiologists. But these latter events need not concern us here since the items mentioned under our three headings will suffice to demonstrate the seriousness and difficulty of the problems and perplexities I want to describe in this chapter.

To begin with, each of the above three accounts of what happened at the precise time of 2.56 p.m. states how something was done. One prepares for a turn by signalling; one signals by raising one's arm; and one raises one's arm by having certain muscle movements take place. Now these are different accounts. Are they different accounts of the same happening or are they accounts of different happenings? Do we or do we not, in these three accounts, have three actions described? And if we have three different actions, which of these actions is the one for which a causal explanation in terms of character and/or anything else is to be given? Here I should like to offer some preliminary considerations in order to bring out the force of these problems.

(a) Let me begin by considering the first pair of descriptions of what occurred: signalling and raising one's arm. On the surface it is implausible to say that signalling and raising one's arm are two distinct occurrences. When one signals a turn, one raises one's arm; but raising one's arm is not the cause of one's signalling and neither is it an event that precedes the latter event. If it were, two occurrences would be distinguishable, one following the other. Surely it would be incorrect to say that when one raises one's arm, as one prepares to make a turn, it will not be true that one will have signalled unless and until certain other events have occurred, e.g. the recognition by other drivers on the road that one was about to execute a turn. For whether or not this does follow the raising of one's arm, one has signalled. If other drivers fail to recognize the raising of one's arm as signalling, they have failed to recognize what is being done, and even if there are no other drivers on the road who might recognize or fail to recognize what is being done, a person who raises his arm in that way is nonetheless signalling. Similarly, even if after raising one's arm in a signalling manoeuvre, one does not proceed to make the turn, one has nonetheless signalled. In raising one's arm one signals—there is only one occurrence—for

20

one does not raise one's arm in order to signal in the way in which one turns the ignition key in order to drive one's car out of the garage and on to the road. In the latter case two things are being done, one following the other; in the former one and only one occurrence is taking place.

But raising one's arm is one thing—according to some philosophers this would be described as a 'mere' bodily movement—and signalling is something else again. Hence the familiar move that signalling is no mere item of 'overt behaviour' (whatever *that* means), but this together with something else, a mental occurrence, a motive.[1] To this view there is the familiar objection that it obliterates the distinction between action and action from a motive, but there are other considerations of at least equal weight. On such a view, the motive being a private mental occurrence, it is strictly speaking incorrect to say that we can ever observe someone signalling. Further, this move would also seem to obliterate the distinction between signalling inadvertently (one raises one's arm to point to some object of interest to one's passenger and, in reply to the accusation made subsequently, 'You signalled!' replies not that one had not done this at all, but rather that one did not mean or intend to do so) and signalling when this is an intentional action. In any case the appeal to a motive to mark off the action from the so-called 'mere' bodily movement suffers from just those obscurities and confusions that mark

[1] Cf. Prichard's discussion and rejection of this view, held by H. W. B. Joseph, in the former's *Moral Obligation*, pp. 131 ff., more recently revived by W. J. Rees in 'Moral Rules and the Analysis of "Ought"', *The Philosophical Review*, 1953.

and surround the term 'motive' itself; and until this term has been properly elucidated the account of the difference between an action and the 'mere' bodily movement by which one performs the action must remain, at the very least, inadequate.

It may be of interest in this connection to remark upon the game of 'follow the leader' sometimes played by children. The follower must do what the leader does. But what does the leader do? If the leader walks on each cross-line of the pavement, must the follower do this or must he do it in the same way, by executing the same bodily movements, *e.g.* by walking in a crouching manner? Here the rules are indecisive in settling many a controversy that must arise over whether or not the follower has done what the leader has done; good manners or boredom, not common understanding of the criteria of 'same action', will settle this kind of dispute. And yet this is the problem I have posed in connection with our example of signalling. How varied are the bodily movements executed by persons signalling! The bodily movement, however, is one thing, the signalling is something else; yet there are not two consecutive happenings described as 'raising one's arm' and 'signalling'. And neither are there two concurrent happenings described in this way as there are in the case in which, as I turn the ignition key, I also release the hand brake.

(*b*) Let us now consider the relation between 'raising one's arm' and 'such-and-such muscles moving in such-and-such a manner'. Whenever I do anything, something happens, but since indefinitely many things happen when I do anything, only some of which are relevant to my doing, the happening in question must be further delimited. Hence a suggestion sometimes made that doing is really making something happen. If this formula for action is accepted not only the movement of my muscles, as I raise my arm, but also the transmission of nerve impulses and the stimulation of the relevant muscles must be regarded as my doing, for whenever I raise my arm, I do make these things happen. But does 'making X happen' mean doing X? Do I, for example, in making certain muscle movements happen, as I raise my arm, move my muscles?

If we follow our natural temptation and give an affirmative answer to this question, the relation between the happenings cited above in (1) and (2) would seem to be the same as the relation between those cited in (2) and (3): I signal by raising my arm—that is how I do it; and similarly, I raise my arm by moving certain muscles in such-and-such a manner—that is how I do *that*. But this move, tempting as it may be, does not square with our ordinary way of speaking. It seems at least as natural to say, when one raises one's arm, that such-and-such muscle movements take place, whereas ordinarily we should not want to say, when one signals, that one's arm gets raised up or that such-and-such a movement of the arm takes place. Our disinclination to employ such locutions about arm movements in ordinary situations stems from the fact that such locutions carry no implication that the arm movements in question are those performed in the ordinary way, that the agent is not moving his arm, for example, by grasping it by the hand and lifting it by using his other arm. If one raises one's arm, one is not paralysed in that arm, one is able to raise it; but if one's arm gets raised this may be done even in the case of one who does not have the use of his arm. So it is in the case of the locution 'such-and-such muscle movements taking place': unlike 'moving such-and-such muscles' this locution would not seem to carry the implication that such muscle movements are normally under the control of the agent. What this comes down to is that if we say that certain muscle movements take place—this is how the arm gets raised—and this indeed is the account of the proceedings given in the happening described as item (3) above, we are not so much saying what the agent is doing as describing what is taking place. And this consideration presents us with an equally strong temptation to deny that the relation between (2) and (3) is the same as that which holds between (1) and (2).

Yet this does not seem to be decisive. Surely I can move such-and-such muscles in just the way in which I do when I raise my arm! But why not also argue that I can stimulate my muscles in just the way in which they are stimulated when they move in just the way in which they do when I raise my arm? And why stop here, why not say that I can activate just such centres of brain activity that are in point of fact activated when nerve impulses are transmitted in just the way in which they are when muscles are stimulated in just the way in which they are when they move in just the way in which they do move when I raise my arm? Surely this is straining matters beyond belief! Yet I can move the muscles of my arm in just the way I do when I raise my arm—nothing is simpler. All I need do, obviously, is raise my arm; and this is easy as pie.

All of this is indecisive, but my concern at this stage is simply to pose questions. In order to begin the task of dealing with the questions and the problems posed in this chapter, I shall now examine the question 'How does one raise one's arm?'

CHAPTER FOUR

HOW DOES ONE RAISE ONE'S ARM?

CONSIDER the question 'How did you keep your promise?' Clearly it is logically impossible to keep one's promise except by doing something describable not only as the keeping of a promise but also in some other way, perhaps as 'returning the book'. Again, if I stopped my car, the question 'How did you do that?' will not be answered by saying, 'I just stopped it'— that would be no answer but a rude rebuff—but by some such account as, 'I applied the hand-brake' or 'I released the accelerator and depressed the brake pedal'. And if someone wants to know how one does X, whatever X may be, the account of how X is done will consist in describing some action Y such that one can say that one does X by doing Y. Thus one signals by raising one's arm, just as one keeps one's promise, say, by returning a borrowed book and stops the car by applying the hand-brake. Two things need to be noticed in any acceptable answer to questions of the form 'How does one do X?': (a) The answer describes some action Y such that by doing Y one does X, and (b) whatever the relation between X and Y may be, 'X' and 'Y' are not synonymous descriptions. One signals by raising one's arm, but 'signalling' and 'raising one's arm' are not synonymous since, if they were,

26

the explanation that one signals by raising one's arm would degenerate into the absurdly trivial utterance that one signals by signalling.

One of the questions posed in the preceding chapter was whether or not the relation between signalling and raising one's arm is like that between raising one's arm and making one's muscles move in such-and-such a manner. This much, of course, is true: I cannot signal except by having my arm extended in a certain way (I assume for simplicity's sake that signals are only given manually) and that I cannot raise my arm except by having certain muscles move in such-and-such a manner. But if the relations between these pairs of happenings are similar, then, just as one answers the question 'How does one signal?' by describing some action that one does (one raises one's arm), so one will answer the question 'How does one raise one's arm?' by describing some action that one does, *e.g.* one moves such-and-such muscles in such-and-such a way. In both cases one does something (signalling, raising one's arm) by *doing* something (raising one's arm, moving such-and-such muscles). I shall argue that both the answer and the question itself are wholly misconceived.

Instead of dealing directly with this question, however, I shall now consider a matter that may seem to be wholly unrelated to it, but which connects in an important way with some of the issues involved in our question. Consider the case of someone in full possession of the use of his limbs, fully alert to what it is that he is doing as he drives his car, and playing a game of saying what he is doing as he manipulates the controls. Among other things he says, 'Now I am raising my arm.' On what basis, if any, does he make this statement? The natural temptation is to argue that he must have some basis for his statement, otherwise he could not meet the challenge 'How do you know?' and could not therefore be said to be justified in saying as he did, 'Now I am raising my arm.' Of course we can easily imagine circumstances in which a person might have doubts as to whether or not he is raising his arm. A person fogged with sleep, relearning the use of his limbs after having suffered paralysis, or being subjected to so-called muscular co-ordination experiments might well be in doubt as to just what his limbs are doing and just where they might be. If my arm has been in a cramped position (the 'pins and needles' feeling has not yet, but will in a moment, come to me) I may not be able to say where my arm is unless I look at it or touch it with the hand of my other normal arm. If I am foggy with sleep I shall have to jerk myself into wakefulness; if I am relearning the use of my arm I may have to look at it, and so on— in order to be able to meet the challenge 'How do you know?' But what justification, given the normal use and condition of my arm and my body, do I need?

A familiar doctrine is that we must have some basis for such statements about our limbs, namely, our kinaesthetic sensations, otherwise we shall have to look and see in order to be able to say where they are and how they are moving. On this view such sensations constitute a sort of continuum corresponding to and connected with the continuous movement of one's arm as, for example, it moves through a region of space from one position to another. For every discernible movement and position of one's arm, there must

28

be certain sensory data—how else could one tell without looking?—hence there is, corresponding to the
continuous sweep of one's arm, a complicated series
of kinaesthetic sensations. It is worth noting that the
motives for this talk about kinaesthetic sensations are
similar to those that have led philosophers to speak
of visual spaces constituted by complex series of
visual sense-data or sensa; for here too it is alleged
that one locates the position and movements of bodies
one observes by means of sensations one receives
through the stimulations of the retina, hence corresponding to the continuous movement of, say, a tennis
ball in space there will be a continuum of sensation
constituting a private space and related in some
peculiar and problematic way to the public space in
which the object is moving. Hence each of us is able
to make statements about the position and movement
of an observed object in public physical space on the
basis of the visual (ignoring for the moment tactual)
sensations that constitute a sort of private visual space.

It would carry us too far afield to explore the details
of this doctrine of private visual (or tactual) spaces.
Here I shall comment only on the doctrine that we
are able to tell the movement and position of our limbs
on the basis of our kinaesthetic sensations and in doing
so merely state in outline some of the decisive points
made by Wittgenstein in his discussion of this view.[1]

What in fact are the sensations one has as one
moves one's arm? If there are such sensations—a

[1] In *Philosophical Investigations*, Pt. II, Sec. viii. For a more extended presentation of Wittgenstein's very brief and cryptic argument, see my paper, 'My Kinaesthetic Sensations Advise Me . . .'
in *Analysis*, December 1957.

whole continuum of sensations, varying in character from one to the next, each corresponding to every discriminable position as one's arm makes a sweep, no argument is necessary. But here we do have an argument—there *must* be such sensations, and one should ask, therefore, why any argument is needed in order to establish this point. Is it that our sensations elude us, that we need to look for them and run the risk of failing to find them? But what would 'eluding us', 'looking for' and 'failing to find' mean as applied to sensations? If there are such sensations, how can we be in doubt about them? And why not, then, say what they are straight off without argument of any sort? The use of an *argument* to establish the occurrence of a continuum of kinaesthetic sensations should warn us against possible conceptual confusions. And in point of fact the sensations we have are altogether different from the alleged continuum—they are usually slight, relatively diffuse, a feeling of tension here and there. Ironically Wittgenstein asks, 'Can these sensations advise me of the movement?' This is not to say that one cannot be advised in special circumstances of bodily movements. If my arm has gone somewhat numb because of some injury, a sharp pain might advise me of its movement. But in my present case there is very little that I have in the form of sensation when I move my arm, and can *these* advise me? Think of the wide variety of sensations I must have if they are to advise me of my bodily movements—every little movement must have a sensation all its own! But assume all of this that flies in the face of the plainest experience, that one tells from one's sensation—if one does, it must be possible to explain this 'telling'.

And how can one explain 'telling from one's sensation' unless one can describe the sensation? At this point one may be tempted to say that these sensations are indefinable, but this move, while unassailable, is immune from further attack only because it is unintelligible. But if 'telling from one's sensation' is intelligible, it is possible to explain its meaning—to teach one how to use this expression; and if the use of this expression can be taught, it is possible to misunderstand it, and hence there are criteria of its having been properly understood. It is no answer to say, 'One knows what "one's sensation" means and one knows that "telling" means, so one knows that "telling from one's sensation" means.' Elsewhere Wittgenstein remarks upon the utter futility of this kind of move.[1] Surely the only criteria one could have would need to be bound up with the description given of the sensations. Suppose, for example, that a safe-cracker is teaching his art to his aspiring son. At one point in the course of instruction he says, 'One can tell from the sensation one has as one twirls the dial on the safe that the tumblers in the lock have fallen' and if asked to explain this 'telling from the sensation', he might well reply that one feels a click of metal against metal in one's finger-tips—this is how one tells. Such a reply is intelligible. One already knows what kind of sensation this is and so one can learn the use of 'telling from one's sensation' in this case. But suppose our safecracker resorted to indefinables: 'It is a *je ne sais quois* feeling one has at the tip of one's finger.' This is at best an arty dodge or a joke, no

---

[1] Cf. his discussion of 'He has the same as I have' in *Philosophical Investigations*, § 350, p. 111e.

instruction at all. Hence not any account will do. It will not do to say, 'The sensation one gets, and this is how one tells that the tumblers fall, is the sensation one gets when the tumblers fall.' Yet this is precisely the sort of move philosophers make in their account of the sensations constituting our so-called visual space; and this sort of account, interestingly enough, Wittgenstein himself had given in his earlier acount of kinaesthetic sensations in the *Blue Book*: the sensations in question are just those that one gets when one's arm moves in such-and-such a manner. His reply in the *Investigations* is decisive:

'Suppose I want to describe a feeling to someone and I tell him, "Do *this* and then you'll get it" and I hold my arm or head in a particular way. Now is this a description of a feeling? And when shall I say that he has understood what feeling I meant?—He will have to give a *further* description of the feeling afterwards.

' "Do *this*, and you'll get it." Can't there be a doubt here? Mustn't there be one, if it is a feeling that is meant?' (pp. 185e–186e).

If all we can say about our alleged kinaesthetic sensations is that they are the ones one gets when one moves one's arm, there must be a doubt that anyone has understood what it means to say that one tells from one's kinaesthetic sensations that one moves one's arm; just as there would always be a doubt in the case of our safecracker example that his son had understood if all that could be done, in explanation of 'One tells from the sensation that one has when the tumblers fall', is to say that the sensation one gets is the sensation one gets when the tumblers fall. In short, unless the alleged kinaesthetic sensations can be described, we have no way of understanding what anyone means when he says that he can tell from his kinaesthetic sensations that his arm is moving.

No doubt one has sensations as one moves one's arm; and if one's arm were anaesthetized, so that one lacked all feeling in the arm, one might not be able to tell the position and movement of one's arm. From this it simply does not follow that one tells on the basis of the sensations one normally has—that one's sensations justify the telling, *that* being how one knows. All that does follow is that where sensation is absent, circumstances are altered in such a way that one is not able to tell, and whether this is a logical matter having to do with evidence or with some other matter that affects our ability to tell is in no way prejudged by this simple, familiar fact. Why then should one be inclined, as no doubt all of us are, on first thought, to suppose that it shows that one's sensations advise one of the position and movement of one's arm? The answer is to be found in the philosophical conception of sensations conveyed by the term 'kinaesthetic sensation'.

The picture is an old and a persuasive one. Each of us receives sensations from our bodies just as we receive sensations from external objects through the stimulation of our sensory organs. These sensations constitute evidence for the statements we make about the related objects—our bodies and their movements in the one case, and the 'external' objects about us in the other. But if they are evidence, we can describe that evidence without begging the question of the existence of that for which ostensibly they are evidence. We can, in other words, treat such sensations as private objects, describable wholly in terms of their intrinsic characteristics and relations to one another without borrowing in any way from the language we apply to bodies, our own and those without us. Indeed that language about objects is now thought to be in some way 'dependent' upon the language of sensations, if not wholly explicable in terms of that language then explicable in terms of the characteristics and relations disclosed by our sensations, which are statable in an ideally purified sensation language, together with, as Broad put it, certain 'categorial' notions such as 'cause', 'substance' and the like. Given such a conception, it seems plausible to speak of visual space, tactual space, kinaesthetic space—various arrays of sensations exhibiting the formal properties of points or volumes in space—'spaces' upon the basis of which the more problematic claims we make about bodies in space, our own and those without us, are in some manner grounded or groundable.

Now the curious feature of the attempt to describe the alleged kinaesthetic sensations we have when we move our limbs (and this same difficulty appears in the familiar but unsuccessful attempts by both phenomenalists and non-phenomenalists alike to give an account of our so-called visual or tactual space in terms that are wholly free from any reference to objects in space) is that it appears impossible to say what the kinaesthetic sensations are without introducing just such locutions as 'sensations we have when we do such-and-such'. Wittgenstein himself had observed, in the *Blue Book*, that we have to resort to just such locutions in order to describe the alleged

kinaesthetic space, language which implies the existence and movements of the relevant portions of our
bodies. But at the time, Wittgenstein put this curious
fact down to the fact that our ordinary language is,
as he then put it, 'slightly cumbrous' and even 'sometimes misleading'. 'We are handicapped,' he complained, 'by having to describe . . . sensations by
means of terms for physical objects . . . We have to use
a roundabout description of our sensations' (p. 52).
What Wittgenstein seems not to have recognized in
1933-34, when he dictated what came to be called
'The Blue Book', is that this circumstance, far from
being either curious or a reflection upon the misleading
character of ordinary language, is symptomatic of a
fatal weakness involved in the conception of such sensations. For on that conception, the sensations are
viewed as private objects describable ideally in a
language from which all connection with concepts of
public objects have been stripped. At that time, it
seemed as if our common language gets in the way of
our clear access to such sensations—if only we could
describe what each of us has as sensations without
having to drag in references to objects in the accounts
we give! But the trouble is much deeper than this—
the failure to recognize that the language of sensations
we actually employ is of necessity parasitic upon a
speech that is employed in practical contexts (in the
Investigations, the term 'language-game' is employed),
in which persons are engaged in their dealings with
each other and with the various exigencies that arise
in their familiar sorts of conduct. It is then no accident
that pains are describable as they are as sharp, dull,
located in one's arms or legs—these are features of

pains that come not by way of addition to the character of our pain experiences but by way of explanation of the sort of experiences pains are—the very terms employed to describe our pains reveal the logical connection between the concept of pain and the concepts we apply to both our bodies and to ordinary objects.[1] And so it is with our bodily sensations as we move our arms—our descriptions are of necessity descriptions that are bound up with the language of familiar and public objects—a feeling of tension here, or there, and so on. It is then a mistake of a fundamental character with respect to the concept of a sensation to suppose that sensations can be described in complete independence of our common concepts of bodies, our own or those outside our skins.

Yet this is precisely what the expression 'kinaesthetic sensations' is commonly designed to convey; for they are, as one dictionary definition informs us, sensations that arise from, and inform us of, our moving limbs because they issue somehow from our muscles and joints. We are, then, to think of them as internal signals issuing from our members as they move and describable in their own terms, without reference of any sort to the limbs, muscles and joints that are set into operation. Just as the sounds of a motor which are describable without reference of any sort to motors inform a skilled mechanic of the condition of the motor—that the spark-plugs are fouled or that the timing of the explosions in the cylinders is off, so each of us has learned to associate the private messages received from our limbs, messages having

[1] It is then no accident that Wittgenstein concludes his discussion as he does in *Philosophical Investigations*, Pt. II, Sec. viii.

their own intrinsic characteristics each peculiar to every specific movement of every specific member of our bodies, with the position and movement of those limbs—no small feat indeed for the young infant! And to this conception, the challenge 'Describe these sensations!' is both relevant and decisive.

But there is another facet of this picture of the proceedings that is of immediate relevance to the question with which I began this chapter, namely, 'How does one move one's arm?' The doctrine of kinaesthetic sensations is designed, to be sure, not as an answer to *this* question, but to the question 'How does one know the position and movement of one's limbs?' But the answer it provides is an answer to the question 'How does one know, say, the movement of one's arm when it gets raised?' And nothing in the account usually given of the manner in which 'kinaesthetic sensations' are alleged to advise us of the movement of one's arm implies that one moves one's arm at all. There is surely a difference between moving one's arm and having it moved, say, by someone else. If then kinaesthetic sensations advise one, when one moves one's arm, that the arm is getting moved, how can one tell without observing one's arm move that one is *raising* one's arm? Surely one would have to be aware of something one *does*, and what can this be? If the doing is simply the raising of one's arm, why not say that one needs no sensation to tell us that one is moving one's arm, no inner signals of any sort, that one is able to tell simply because one is able to *make* the proposition 'I am raising my arm' true? Why not, in other words, regard the ability to raise one's arm not as a skill learned by associating inner signals with observed

37

motions of one's arm but as a primitive ability acquired when the mechanism of the body reaches a certain state of maturity? And why, therefore, be seduced by the question 'How do you know?' and attempt to offer evidence in terms of alleged kinaesthetic sensations, thus subscribing to all of the muddles involved in this philosophical picture of bodily sensations, rather than rebuff the question as wholly misconceived by 'I just raise my arm—that is how I can say without observing its movement that it is in fact moving—because I can make it true that I am raising my arm, I can say straight off without observation of inner or outer entities of any sort.'

Yet this answer stands in conflict with the long-standing logician's conception of a proposition. A proposition, so conceived, is defined as something that is either true or false, depending upon whether or not it agrees with some antecedent 'reality' or 'state of affairs' and with respect to which asserting and denying, hoping and expecting come by way of addition to the proposition through the adjunction of certain inner mental processes. If then I assert p, whatever p may be, what I assert, the proposition, is true if and only if there is some state of affairs—independent of my assertion—the fact. In all of these cases of asserting, hoping, expecting, praying, there is either success or failure (one's assertion is true or false, one's hopes are realized or not, one's expectations are or are not met, and so on), but each of us is reduced in respect to these mental processes to the rôle of spectator, contemplating the scene or awaiting the outcome of events—to be sure, doing something now by performing some mental event of asserting, hoping, expecting, etc., but helpless in our contemplation before the movement of events into the future upon whose course and direction our success or failure depends. But why not elucidate a proposition as something that can be *made* true or false, whether by events over which we may have no control or by ourselves in what we do? How am I able to say what the movement and position of my arm is when I move it? Here I need no evidence in the form of sensations to advise me of the state of affairs consisting of the movement of my arm —because I am able to make that state of affairs true, *i.e.* I am able to move my arm (and this is *all* that I do), I am able to say how my arm is moving. And if this is so, 'How does one move one's arm?' is as mis-conceived as the demand for evidence—'How do you know that your arm is moving?—since, when I move my arm, there is no Y that I do by which this X (moving my arm) is done. In short, if what I have suggested is true, then the relation between signalling and raising my arm (I do the former by doing the latter) is quite different from the relation between raising one's arm and the contraction of muscles, since in the latter case I raise my arm not by doing anything else at all. I simply exercise my primitive ability to raise my arm. Thus it is that our questions, 'How does one raise one's arm?' and 'How does one know that one's arm moves as it does when one raises it?' may be far more closely related than appears to be the case at first sight.

It may be objected that this is unfair and that the logician's picture of a proposition does not reduce one, in the case of one's own action, to the utter helplessness of a spectator. If one raises one's arm—call this 'Y'—

one does something, X (perhaps one wills, or moves one's muscles, or what not), and if one says, 'Now I am raising my arm', the fact that the arm is rising is not something that comes to pass in the way in which events in the interior of the sun do. In the latter case we must await the course of nature since these events are not under our control, but in our case it is by X-ing that Y comes to pass; and that one is X-ing is something that one knows and does. Hence, whether or not Y occurs is not a matter before which we must remain in utter helplessness. Yet this reply creates more problems than it solves. What is the Y? Is it the rising of one's arm or one's raising of one's arm? And are we to say that one knows one is doing the latter because one knows that one is doing an X that somehow produces the former, *i.e.* the rising of one's arm, the truth of which is evidenced by sensations? Leaving aside all of the difficulties involved in knowing or telling from one's sensations, what one really does (and this would seem to be the more accurate way of speaking on this picture of the proceedings) is X; it is not that one Y's (raises one's arm), but really that Y^1 occurs (the rising of one's arm). In any case how does one know that one X's, whatever this may be? There is a difference between saying that one X's and that an X-ish event occurs, corresponding to the difference between saying that one raises one's arm and saying that one's arm is rising. And how do I know that I am X-ing, whatever this X may be? Surely not by contemplating some occurrence taking place in me; for this can only assure me that an X-ish sort of event is happening in me, not that I am X-ing. Are we not driven to conceding that one can say correctly, 'I am X-ing' simply because one can make the statement 'I am X-ing' true; that is to say, one can be correct in saying that one X's, simply by X-ing? Here it may be objected that one must know, be in a position to tell or be aware of the fact, that one is X-ing—it is not enough that one is X-ing, one must also have knowledge of this fact. But if the X-ing is something mental that one does, what does the thought involved in 'knowing that one is X-ing' (similarly with 'being in a position to tell', 'being aware') convey that is different from the thought that one is doing X? (What does 'I am aware of a pain' mean if it is not a queer way of saying 'I have a pain'?) And if X-ing is not something mental, how can I be aware of it? Must not the same difficulty arise at this point and lead us in an impossible regress? But if one can X and simply by X-ing say correctly that one is X-ing, why not say the same about 'I am raising my arm', where I raise my arm not by doing some other action by which my arm succeeds in getting raised, but simply by raising my arm? In short, why make a move that seems to lead us on into an impossible morass? Why not, therefore, reject both questions, 'How does one raise one's arm?' and 'How does one know that one is raising one's arm?', as wholly misconceived? Why not, in short, stop with 'I am raising my arm' which one can assert not because of evidence one has or a doing one engages in distinct from the raising of one's arm, but because one has this ability to raise one's arm and hence can make true the proposition that one is raising one's arm?

The question posed at the beginning of this chapter seems only to lead to a whole host of further questions. I have been concerned in this discussion to suggest doubts about the propriety of our initial question, and I recognize all too well that what I have said may be unconvincing. It will be necessary therefore to turn to specific types of answers given by philosophers to our question in order to show in detail the incoherence of both the question and the answers.

CHAPTER FIVE

BY WILLING, ONE DOES . . .

CONSIDER the following: Whenever I raise my arm (deliberately, let us say) I bring to pass certain muscle movements—I make these happen. Hence I raise my arm by moving (contracting and expanding) certain muscles of my arm. This, then, is how I raise my arm.

This is a bad argument. We cannot identify what one does with what one makes happen. When I flex the biceps brachii of my arm very many things are brought to pass, made to happen. Nerve impulses are transmitted to the muscles, neural circuits in the brain are opened and closed, protein molecules in the brain are set into oscillation; and many many more things of which I have not the faintest intimation. But let us consider the conclusion on its own merits. Certainly I can contract certain muscles at will. If someone points to the biceps brachii and asks me to flex it, this I can easily do. So it is tempting to say that when I raise my arm, I do so by moving certain muscles *just as* when I signal, I do so by raising my arm.

But how do I move certain muscles? There is a difference between my biceps becoming flexed and *my* flexing my biceps just as there is a difference between my arm getting raised and *my* raising my arm. The

43

flexing of my biceps may occur through no doing of mine (someone might raise my arm and in doing so cause my biceps to be flexed) just as my arm getting raised may be something that happens to me through the action of another person who raises my arm and not through anything I do. And what can the difference be, between the occurrence of a muscle movement in my arm and my moving that muscle, except this, that in the latter case it is by doing something that I bring the muscle movement to pass? In short, if it is sensible to say that I raise my arm by moving certain muscles, it is equally sensible to hold that one moves those muscles by doing something that brings those muscle movements to pass. And what can this latter doing be that has these muscle movements as effect?

Suppose someone points to the biceps brachii and says, 'Flex it!' What must I do in order to comply? Must I say to myself, 'Move, muscle, move!'? If I do this, nothing will happen. Does nothing happen because I do not *mean* it? Then how do I *mean* it? 'Meaning what I say'—is this something I do when I say whatever it is that I do say? Shall we say that I shall mean it only when I *want* my muscle to move? But if I want my biceps to move and stare at it again nothing will happen—I must do something about my want, *i.e.* get what it is that I want. Is it necessary that I set myself—to use Prichard's expression—to move my biceps?[1] But if 'setting myself' means getting ready, putting myself in a state of readiness, again nothing will happen. And if 'setting myself to do' means trying to do or exerting myself to do, then I need do nothing

---

[1] Cf. the essay 'Duty and Ignorance of Fact' in *Moral Obligation*, Oxford, 1949.

of the sort. I do not try to raise my arm unless, *e.g.* it is held down—I simply raise it; and I do not try to flex my biceps unless there is some obstacle to be overcome or some chance of failure.

What then is the difference between my muscles being contracted and my contracting my muscles? A familiar doctrine is that in the latter case I *will* my muscles to move, whereas in the former case there are causes other than the act of volition. So I move my muscles by performing an act of volition which in turn produces a muscle movement.

Grant for a moment that an event labelled an 'act of volition' produces a muscle movement, there is a difference surely between an act of volition occurring and my performing such an act. We saw that there is a difference between the occurrence of a muscle move-ment and my moving that muscle, hence it was that the supposition of acts of volition was invoked. But equally there is a difference between the occurrence of an act of volition and my performing such an act— who can say that volitions may not occur through no doing of the subject, and in consequence, of interior mental events deep within the hidden recesses of the self? If so, willing the muscle movement is not enough, one must will the willing of the muscle movement, and so on *ad infinitum*. Here someone may retort impati-ently: 'When I will a muscle movement, *I* will it and that is the end of the matter; there is no other doing by virtue of which this act of volition gets done—I simply will the movement of the muscle.' But even if this reply were correct it would not serve to explain what an action is as distinguished from a mere hap-pening—it explains the 'action' of raising the arm in terms of an internal action of willing, and hence all it does at best is to change the locus of action. Indeed it invites the view argued by Prichard that, strictly speaking and contrary to the notion conveyed by our ordinary ways of speaking, one does not raise one's arm at all—all one does or can do is *will* and by means of *this* action produce various effects such as the rising of one's arm. In any case if willing is some sort of doing one performs not by means of any other doing (one wills and that is the end of the matter), why not say the same about the movement of one's muscles—one tenses one's biceps and there is no doing by virtue of which the tensing gets done? But the troubles involved in the supposition that there are interior acts of willing go even deeper than this—the doctrine, familiar though it may be, is a mare's nest of confusions.

How shall we describe the alleged action of willing? Surely a description of *this* action independently of the consequence alleged for it—the production of a muscle movement—must be forthcoming. Let us call the act of willing A: then A produces B (a muscle movement), this being taken to be a causal sequence. Now in general if A causes B, a description of A other than that it has the causal property of producing B must be forthcoming, otherwise 'A causes B' degenerates into 'the thing that produces B produces B'. But what description of the act of volition can be offered? If something causes me to jump in fright, jerk my arm, or move my head, 'What caused you to . . .?' is intelligible and answerable. It is no good saying, 'That which caused me to do it', for this is no answer but a bit of rudeness or a feeble attempt at humour. How then shall one describe the act of willing?

It is at this point that the resort to indefinables appears attractive.[1] Willing is *sui generis*, indefinable, a bit of mental self-exertion in which we engage—an activity not capable of further description but different from the wonderings, thinkings, supposings, expectings, picturings, etc. that comprise our mental activities. Yet the appeal to indefinables is a desperate defence that purchases immunity from further attack only at the expense of unintelligibility. Here the kind of objections raised by Wittgenstein against the doctrine of kinaesthetic sensations apply in full force. If all that can be said about the alleged act of volition, by virtue of which a muscle movement is produced, is that it is the sort of thing that produces a muscle movement, there is every uncertainty that anyone has understood what is meant by 'the act of volition'. And if an attempt to rescue this doctrine is made by appealing to something with which, it is alleged, each of us is intimately familiar and hence will have no difficulty in recognizing—the act of volition that produces the muscle movement—the retort must surely be '*What* do I recognize when I recognize an act of volition?' Unless I can recognize this act by having some description in mind that applies to such acts and only to these, it is at best a simple begging of the question to insist that all of us really understand what is being referred to; in fact it is an implied charge of dishonesty directed at those who refuse to give their assent. And in philosophy, when good manners alone

[1] Indeed, this is the move made by Prichard in the essay 'Acting, Willing, Desiring', written in 1945 and published posthumously in *Moral Obligation*, Oxford, The Clarendon Press, 1949. This essay is worth careful reading; in it Prichard abandons his earlier account of 'willing' as setting oneself to do.

stand in the way of the open parade of charges of this sort, there is something seriously amiss in one's thinking.

But the difficulty in this talk about acts of volition is not merely that some account of acts of volition in general is needed, failing which we can only conclude that the expression 'act of volition' can serve no rôle in our discourse, it is equally serious in other respects as well. Let us grant that there is some peculiar mental activity of willing, the causal consequence of which is that certain muscles are contracted and others relaxed as we perform our diverse bodily movements, and let us now ask first of all how it is that we are able to learn how to perform these bodily movements. Surely the act of volition involved in the production of one muscle movement must be distinguished from the act of volition involved in the production of any other. There will then be different acts of volition, v_1, v_2, v_3, etc., which, respectively, move muscles m_1, m_2, m_3, etc. If $v_1 \rightarrow m_1$, $v_2 \rightarrow m_2$, $v_3 \rightarrow m_3$, etc. represent causal relations, then just as m_1, m_2, m_3, etc. are distinguishable, so v_1, v_2, v_3, etc. will needs be different in kind. And if I am to learn how to produce m_1 by performing the act of volition v_1, I must not only recognize the difference between v_1 and other acts of volition that have other effects, I must also recognize the causal relation holding between v_1 and m_1. Now this would seem to imply at least two things: (1) It must be possible to offer a set of characterizations of these acts of volition each different from the other, corresponding to the set of characterizations that can be given surely for the muscle movements m_1, m_2, m_3, m_4, etc. (2) I can only learn from experience that m_1 is produced by v_1, m_2

48

by v_2, m_3 by v_3, and soon, hence unless I suppose myself to have been endowed with superhuman prescience, I must have been surprised or astonished the first time I performed the act of volition v_1 to discover that muscle movement m_1 occurred; and antecedently I should have had no reason for ruling out the possibility that m_2 would not occur—I should have had no reason, for example, to suppose that when I performed that act of volition by which in fact my biceps became flexed, my right leg would not have been raised.

Consider the first of these consequences. Now I can certainly distinguish between muscle movements m_1 and m_2, say, the biceps of my right arm from that of my left arm. But how shall I distinguish between the acts of volition v_1 and v_2 by which these distinct muscle movements are produced? If I produce these muscle movements by performing these acts of volition, this at any rate is something I learn to do, an ability I come to acquire. But if I can learn to do this, I must be able to distinguish between the volitions v_1 and v_2. Surely it must be possible to describe the difference. And if this cannot be done, learning to produce m_1 by producing v_1 and learning to produce m_2 by producing v_2 is impossible. How then shall we describe v_1 as distinguished from v_2? Shall we say that not only are volitions in general indefinable, but that the difference between v_1 and v_2 is also something indefinable? At least, however, the difference must be recognizable. Is it that our vocabulary is inadequate? Then let us introduce words that will enable us to mark the distinction. And now that the words have been introduced, explain how they are to be employed! Is it that we can only *point*—v_1 is *this* thing, the one that one finds one performs when m_1 is produced, v_2 is *that* thing, the one that one finds that one performs when m_2 is produced? But this will do the trick only if I already know what sorts of things to look for and only if it is at least possible for me to go on and describe the difference between v_1 and v_2 independently of the considerations that v_1 produces m_1 and v_2 produces m_2. By pointing one can succeed in explaining the meaning of a term or expression, but only if by doing so one can help fill in a gap or supply the links missing in some initial background understanding we have of that term of expression. But here we do not know where to look or what to find. No background understanding is present. We are told that there are certain things—call them 'acts of volition'—that they are indefinable, and that nothing more can be said about them at all in explaining how this expression 'act of volition' is to be employed. Against *this* background, how can pointing serve to provide any explanation at all of the difference between act of volition$_1$ (call it mental-muscle-doing$_1$) and act of volition$_2$ (mental-muscle-doing$_2$)? To say at this point that the difference itself is indefinable is, surely, to carry philosophical pretension beyond all limits of credulity.

As far as I know philosophers are quite unwilling to pile indefinables upon indefinables in this fulsome manner. Prichard for one, despite his characteristic resort to indefinables, is admirable for an equally characteristic subtlety that leads him to reject such simple-minded answers even though, as he himself recognizes, he must accept a conclusion that is open to objections he cannot meet. Consider the second of the two consequences of the doctrine of acts of volition. That v_1 produces m_1 rather than m_2 is a causal fact; but if so, I should have no reason to suppose, when I first performed the act of volition v_1, that m_1 rather than m_2 would follow; for on this view the statement that, *e.g.* I move the biceps brachii of my right arm by performing the act of volition v_1, rather than the biceps brachii of my left arm or the biceps femoris of my right leg, is justified only on the basis of inductive evidence. Now Prichard holds that an act of volition involves a desire to will whatever it is that one wills, and hence some idea of what the volition is likely to produce. This, however, is impossible since on the first occasions on which I performed v_1 and thereby produced m_1, v_1 would require the thought that I would be doing something that would produce m_1 and by hypothesis I should have no reason to expect what, if anything, v_1 would produce. Prichard is therefore led to the conclusion that an 'act of will requires an idea of something which we may cause if we perform the act', a conclusion—indeed a difficulty —he is unable to avoid.[1]

Prichard's predicament involves a matter of central importance which can be stated quite independently of his insistence that if one is to perform an act of volition, one must be moved by a desire to perform that volition. The important issue is whether or not it is intelligible to speak of an act of volition where the very notion of such an act does not involve a reference to the relevant bodily event. Let the act of volition

[1] *Op. cit.*, pp. 196–7. See also his second thoughts about his earlier notion of 'setting oneself' in the footnotes to his earlier essay, 'Duty and Ignorance of Fact', which appear in the same volume on p. 38.

issue in a muscle movement; then as Prichard himself recognizes, the act must be the willing of that muscle movement, otherwise we should have only inductive grounds for supposing the act to issue in that particular muscle movement. Accordingly we are faced with the following dilemma: If in thinking of v_1 (some particular act of volition) we are of necessity to think of it as the willing of m_1 (some particular muscle movement), then v_1 cannot be any occurrence, mental or physiological, which is causally related to m_1, since the very notion of a causal sequence logically implies that cause and effect are intelligible without any logically internal relation of the one to the other. If on the other hand, we think of v_1 and m_1 as causally related in the way in which we think of the relation between the movements of muscles and the raising of one's arm, then we must conclude that when first we perform v_1 we should have absolutely no reason to suppose that m_1 would in fact ensue. If to avoid this latter consequence we maintain that the thought of the muscle movement enters into the very character of the act of volition (as Prichard puts it, 'the *thinking* enters into the character of the *willing*' (*ibid.*, p. 38)) no description of the act of volition can be given that does not involve an account of the muscle movement, and hence we must abandon the idea that the act of volition v_1 is a cause that produces m_1, the muscle movement. Prichard's predicament is that his conclusion that 'an act of will requires an idea of something which we may cause if we perform the act' is nothing less than self-contradictory.

This then is the logical incoherence involved in the doctrine of acts of volition: Acts of volition are alleged to be direct causes of certain bodily phenomena (whether these be brain occurrences, as Prichard supposed them to be, or muscle movements, as we have been assuming for the sake of argument, is of no matter), just as the latter are causes of the raising of one's arm. For, it is alleged, just as we raise our arms by moving our muscles, so we move our muscles by willing them to move. But no account of the alleged volitions is intelligible that does not involve a reference to the relevant bodily phenomena. And *no* interior cause, mental or physiological, can have this logical feature of acts of volition. Let the interior event which we call 'the act of volition' be mental or physical (*which* it is will make no difference at all), it must be logically distinct from the alleged effect—this surely is one lesson we can derive from a reading of Hume's discussion of causation. Yet nothing can be an act of volition that is not logically connected with that which is willed—the act of willing is intelligible only as the act of willing whatever it is that is willed. In short, there could not be such an interior event like an act of volition since (here one is reminded of Wittgenstein's famous remark about meaning) nothing of that sort could have the required logical consequences.

Let me review the course of the argument in this chapter. The doctrine of acts of volition was introduced, it will be remembered, in order to elucidate the distinction between one's arm rising and one's raising one's arm. The former need involve no doing or action performed by the agent, the latter surely does. But instead of rejecting the question, 'How does one raise one's arm?' by a 'One just does' retort, the reply we considered was 'One raises one's arm by

moving certain muscles.' Here the same question arises
again: How can one distinguish between 'moving
certain muscles' and 'certain muscles getting moved'?
The latter need involve no action on my part at all.
And if it makes sense to ask, 'How does one raise one's
arm?' surely it makes sense to ask, 'How does one
move certain muscles?' Hence the doing required in
order to preserve the distinction between 'moving
certain muscles' and 'certain muscles getting moved'
must be a doing other than the doing described as
'moving certain muscles'. At this point the philosophical doctrine of acts of volition—willings performed
by an agent—appears attractive. By willing, we move
certain muscles; by moving certain muscles we raise
our arm. But the acts of volition in question are the
ill-begotten offspring of the mating of two quite incompatible ideas: the supposition that such acts are
causes, and the requirement that the volitions in
question be the willings of the muscle movements. As
causes, willings are events on a par with other events
including muscle and other bodily movements, with
respect to which the inevitable question must arise
once more: 'How does one perform such an action?'
since after all there is the distinction to be preserved
between 'performing a willing' and 'a willing occurring'.
But if to avoid the threatened regress of 'willing a
willing' and 'willing the willing of a willing' and so on,
one rejects the question and questions the intelligibility
of such locutions as 'willing a willing', the willing in
question can only be understood as 'the willing of a
muscle movement'. If so, the willing in question cannot
be a cause of the muscle movement, since the reference to the muscle movement is involved in the very

description of the willing. In that case to say that one moves certain muscles by willing them to move is not to give any causal account at all. But if this is so, what can it mean to say that one wills a muscle movement—since the willing in question cannot possibly be any interior occurrence in which one engages? If it is intelligible at all it means simply that one moves a muscle. In that case, the alleged elucidation of the statement that one moves certain muscles (in raising one's arm) by willing them to move degenerates into something that is no elucidation at all, namely, that one moves certain muscles by moving them. And if this is so, to say that one wills the movement of certain muscles is not to *answer* the question, 'How does one move those muscles?', it is in fact to *reject* it. If this is the outcome, why not refuse to plunge into the morass and reject the initial question, 'How does one raise one's arm?', by saying, 'One just does'? If, on the other hand, 'willing a muscle movement' does *not* mean 'moving a muscle', what on earth can it possibly mean? Surely, it is an understatement to say that the philosophical talk about acts of volition involves a mare's nest of confusions!

It is not my contention that the doctrine of volitions is designed to answer only those questions I have raised so far. It is of course true that frequently this doctrine is also invoked in order to give some account of the difference between action that is voluntary and action that is not. Nor do I deny the legitimacy of our familiar use of such locutions as 'acting willingly', 'doing something of one's own will', 'acting wilfully', and so on. But these are matters to be examined as the present argument develops, in their own right and at the proper time.

CHAPTER SIX

PHYSIOLOGICAL HAPPENINGS
AND BODILY ACTIONS

HUME once complained about the careless procedure of philosophers who all too frequently, as he put it, began their discourses on morals with the familiar copulation 'is' and then without explanation or justification employed the quite different locution 'ought' (*A Treatise of Human Nature*, Bk. III, Pt. I, Sec. 2. See the concluding paragraph). But here too we seem to have a gap that needs to be bridged between things that happen, get done, and things that are done by persons when they raise their arms or perform any of the very many sorts of actions of which they are capable. And here, too, Moore's open question technique comes to mind (*Principia Ethica*, Ch. I). A very great number of physiological events take place, happen, get done when one raises one's arm; but it not only makes sense to ask whether these things are things that one does, it is in fact questionable that this is the case. If so, we cannot identify what happens, gets done, with what a person does. Here, corresponding to the familiar gaps that have plagued philosophers, not only in morals but also in aesthetics and in many another field of philosophy, is the gap between matters of physiological happening and matters of human action. And here as elsewhere the appearance of a gap is symptomatic of conceptual confusion.

In the present chapter I shall focus attention upon the question whether or not matters of physiological happenings can also be described legitimately as matters of action, things done by the agent. But first a word of warning is in order to guard against a familiar *a priorism* with respect to matters of physiology.

The problem of how we may construe matters of bodily happening, whether these be the movements of muscles or limbs, as matters of human action has seemed to some philosophers to throw doubt upon the common assumption of physiologists that a complete causal account of such bodily happenings in terms of antecedent physiological occurrances is possible. Prichard, for example, remarks that if we are to think that by willing we expect some change in our bodies 'we are implying the idea that in doing so, we are butting into, or interfering with, the physical system' (*Moral Obligation*, p. 193). For the act of volition, the willing, is construed as a causal factor in the absence of which in the given circumstances the bodily movement would not have occurred. And this seems to imply that in cases of human action there are gaps in the chain of physiological causes which are filled in by the doings of agents; whether these be willings or any other instances of causal efficacy of minds is of no matter. Now there is undoubtedly a difference between a matter of physiological happening and a bodily movement that is correctly describable as something done by the agent. We must be on our guard, however, against the conclusion we are too often invited to draw, namely, that the claims and aspirations of physiologists must be rejected since whenever a person acts, no complete physiological explanation of the bodily happening is possible. This surely is *a priorism* at its worst, recognition of which should warn us that there is something radically wrong with the picture we have in mind of the manner in which the gap between physiological happening and doing is to be bridged. According to this picture (often quite explicitly drawn in diagrammatic representations of the bodily mechanism in order to explain, for the benefit of laymen and children, how it is that human beings perceive and act in response to stimuli), the human body is an elaborate mechanism, in which extremely fine and complex controls in the nervous system determine the character of the bodily responses to stimuli from without. So far we have only the picture of an elaborate machine. In order, then, to provide verisimilitude, to give us the impression that the mechanism is that of a human being, we are invited to think of the controls in the central nervous system as somehow manipulated; and this is sometimes done by adding to the diagram, by representing a human-like figure pulling levers and pushing buttons. Prichard's willings are precisely the equivalent of these manipulating activities and, like the sort of diagram I have described, imply that there is a gap in any possible physiological explanation of the observable physiological happenings—the movements of our limbs, the blinkings of eyes, the movements of lips and tongue, and so on. What has happened in effect is that the attempt to bridge the gap between physiological happening and human doing has been made only by introducing another gap, this one in the physiological chain of causes.

The course of western philosophy is littered with the relics of philosophic doctrines that have attempted to legislate what science can or cannot do. The physiologist who envisages the possibility of a complete physiological explanation of bodily happenings surely has history on his side. Before we reject the possibility of such explanations we could do far worse than re-examine the model of the proceedings, a model that threatens once more a clash between philosophy and science. On this model, physiological happenings are construed as doings only by means of the peculiar order of causes involved—a happening is also a doing if and only if it is produced in a certain way, *e.g.* by willings—and, as we have seen, this approach, quite independently of its dubious *a priorism*, is less than auspicious.

Let us look more closely at the following: 'One raises one's arm by contracting certain muscles—this is how one does it.' This implies, of course, that one's muscles are under one's immediate control, that one causes one's arm to rise by moving one's muscles just as one causes the door to unlock by turning the key in the lock. On this picture of the proceedings it is the interior bodily events—certain muscle movements—that are under our immediate control; by moving those muscles we cause the arm to rise. I want to argue that this is a mistake.

Suppose this picture to be true. Then surely I must know which muscles to move. If I cause my arm to rise by moving certain muscles, just as I cause the door to unlock by turning the key in the lock, then just as I can give a true account of the bodily movement I perform in the latter case so I must be able to give a true account of something I do in the former case. When I turn the key in the lock, I may know very little if anything about the mechanism of locks or the manner in which keys inserted and turned in locks produce their familiar effect, but surely I can tell without inspecting or observing what I am doing, that I am executing a twisting manoeuvre with my hand as I firmly hold the key in the lock. But what true account of the movement of the muscles can I give? What I know about the muscle movements, involved in the raising of my arm is very little indeed; and must I know *anything* about these muscle movements in order to raise my arm? But if I need know nothing about the physiology of arm movements, how is it possible for me to have learned how to raise my arm? For on the present view I can raise my arm only by doing something that causes my arm to rise, just as I can unlock the door only by turning the object called 'a key' in the thing commonly described as a lock. So I must be aware of what I am doing in the former case just as I am aware of what I am doing in the latter. Must I learn the physiology of arm movements before I can get my arm to rise in the air? If there is a parallel between causing the door to unlock by turning the key in the lock and causing my arm to rise by moving certain muscles, I should be utterly helpless in the matter of getting my arm to rise in the air until I knew which muscles to move—just as a child is utterly helpless when confronted by a locked door, until it knows what action to perform in order to get the door to unlock. The whole idea that one causes one's arm to rise in the air by manipulating certain internal bodily pulleys and levers is an unwitting piece of philosophical humour.

Does this mean that one cannot move those muscles that do get moved, and in the very precise way in which it happens, when one raises one's arm? Not at all! Indeed, nothing is easier: all one need do is simply raise one's arm! Does this mean that any physiological happening, anything of this kind that gets done, is a case of an action, a doing? Not at all. Does this mean that the view that the contraction of muscles causes the elevation of the arm must be rejected, that it is the other way around since the raising of the arm causes the muscles to contract? Indeed not!

I remarked that nothing is easier than to move those muscles that do get moved in just the way in which they are moved when one raises one's arm, but here we must guard ourselves against misunderstanding. Suppose someone tells me, 'Move those muscles that do get moved in just the way in which they are moved when you raise your arm.' What is he telling me to do? Is he telling me merely to do this—move those muscles in that particular way, and nothing else? In that case my natural retort would be 'Which muscles do you mean?' And if he replies, 'Never mind which muscles they are, just move them in just the way in which . . .', what on earth is he asking me to do? Is this merely a queer way of telling me to raise my arm? But in that case he does not want me merely to move those muscles, since the only way I can oblige is by raising my arm. Certainly I can get those muscles to move in that way by raising my arm, but equally well I can do it by grasping my arm and raising it just as in the case of an idle motor I can get the pistons to move up and down by manually operating the crankshaft. In ordinary circumstances and uttered out of the blue, so to speak, we should have difficulty in understanding someone who says, 'Move those muscles that do get moved in just the way in which they are moved when you raise your arm.'

Nevertheless, we can imagine circumstances in which this would be quite intelligible. Imagine someone teaching me something of the physiology of the arm: He shows me how the arm structure rises when this muscle contracts, that one relaxes, and so on. He shows me, in other words, how the muscles operate when I raise my arm. Now he connects electrodes to each of these muscles and arranges them in such a way that two meter needles will come together at a given point when these muscles are brought into play in the way described. When the muscles move in the way in which they move when I lower my arm, the needles will behave differently. I then learn how to bring the needles together, how to bring them apart, and so on, and I come to be able to read what is going on in my muscles by watching the movements of the needles, just as a mechanic can read what is going on in a motor by watching the results recorded on his test instruments. If under these circumstances, I am told, 'Move those muscles that do get moved in just the way in which they are moved when you raise your arm', I can comply only by bringing the meter needles together, and this I can do only by raising my arm. Here the instruction is intelligibly different from 'Raise your arm'. For suppose that someone unfamiliar with the experiment watches me and notices that my instructor is satisfied every time I raise my arm in response to his 'Move those muscles that do get moved in just the way in which . . .'; he may know that I can do what I must do only by raising my arm, but he will have no further knowledge of what I am required to do.

In special circumstances, the above being only one imaginable case, I can perform the required muscle movements that do take place normally when I raise my arm. But in such cases I do not raise the arm by moving those muscles—I move the muscles by raising the arm. The example should make it clear that my raising my arm is not the effect of some immediate interior bodily doing of mine. I get my muscles to move in the required way by getting the needles to move in a certain way and I do the latter by raising my arm. I do not calculate in any way how to move my arm by doing something that produces it; what occupies my attention is the movement of the needles and what this means for me. In short, the whole picture of bodily actions, such as the movement of our limbs, according to which these are produced by interior performances in which we engage, whether these be muscle movements or anything else, is a caricature of the actual situation. For similar considerations will apply equally well to other candidates for the title of 'things immediately done by us' and which allegedly in their turn produce the motions of our limbs, whether these be the stimulation of the muscle fibres, the excitation of brain centres or what have you. We do not move our limbs by manipulating any sorts of interior levers or pulleys within the body.

It should be clear now that not every physiological happening in the chain of causes that issue in the motion of one's arm is a case of something done. For only in very special circumstances can such a happening be described as an action. Equally well, the contention that in such special circumstances the happening in question is an action accomplished by raising one's arm, in no way does violence to the familiar matter of physiological fact, namely, that such happenings are causes, not effects, of the motion of one's arm. Such cases are quite different from the one cited earlier in which one raises one's arm by lifting it by means of the other arm—by doing this the arm is flaccid as it is lifted and in the process of being lifted certain muscles will be moved, just as in the case of a motor one can reverse the causal sequence of the transmission of the motion of a piston to the crankshaft, by turning the crankshaft manually and forcing the pistons to move in the cylinders of the motor. In the very special case I have elaborated, in order to illustrate the fact that one can be said to move one's muscles by raising one's arm, one performs the *action* of raising one's arm. To say that one moves certain muscles by raising one's arm, is not to say that the physiological happening described as 'muscle movements' is produced by the physiological happening described as 'the elevation of one's arm'. To suppose that it is the same thing is to confound what we have been at pains to emphasize, namely, that physiological happenings are not to be identified with human action. That I can be said to move certain muscles by raising my arm leaves unimpaired the matter of physiological fact that it is the motion of these muscles that causes the motion of the arm. Finally, it should be clear that no attempt to bridge the gap between the physiological happening described as the movement of one's arm and the action described as moving one's arm by any device such as the introduction of causes, mental or physiological, will do. One does not raise one's arm by performing another doing which has the motion of one's arm as effect—one simply raises one's arm.

CHAPTER SEVEN

LEARNING AND PHYSIOLOGY

IT should be abundantly clear by now that the query 'How do I raise my arm?' is wholly misconceived. In raising my arm I am performing an action. There may be interior bodily occurrences that cause the arm to rise; indeed, if what physiologists tell us is true, this must be granted. But the elevation of the arm—the rising of the arm—is one thing, the doing or the action of raising the arm is something else again; and whatever the interior causes of the elevation of the arm may be, it is not by any interior doing, mental or bodily, that I succeed in raising my arm. 'How do I signal?' is a fair question, the answer to which is given by 'By raising my arm.' But in normal circumstances there is no doing of any sort by virtue of which I raise my arm. I simply raise my arm and, in doing this, exercise a primitive ability. How do I know that I am raising my arm, exercising this ability? This question too is misconceived. I do not surmise that I am raising my arm on the basis of any evidence at all; neither bodily sensations nor observation of the arm movement advise me of my action. Nor do I surmise that I am succeeding in raising my arm by knowing that I am doing something likely to have this action as its outcome. I simply make true the proposition that I am raising my arm. But how do I know that I am making this proposition true? Making this proposition true, however, is just raising one's arm, for it is this that makes it true that I am raising my arm. 'How do I know that I am making the proposition true?' is our old improper question in disguise. In short, both questions, 'How do I raise my arm?' and 'How do I know that I am raising my arm?', must be rejected. They are prompted by confusion and misunderstanding.

It is worth commenting on the misleading use, by psychologists, of terms like 'learning' and 'skill' in connection with the acquisition and exercise of what I have described as the primitive ability to raise one's arm. Does a child learn to raise its arm? Certainly its movements are at first random, haphazard. But when it is able to raise its arm, say in order to grasp the rattle suspended above its crib, has it learned to raise its arm? And does it then have a skill—a motor-skill, to use a favourite term? Learning to do something is of course acquiring a skill. A child that learns the operation of opening locked doors acquires a skill in the exercise of which it performs a series of operations. It turns the key in the lock, turns the knob and pulls or pushes, as the case may be. In the case of each of these actions, it performs certain bodily movements. But if raising one's arm were the exercise of a skill, it would make sense to ask, 'How does it do it?' This is how we ordinarily use the word 'skill'. Can the term 'learning' be applied to the acquisition by the infant of this ability to raise its arm? Here one is tempted to give an affirmative reply: after all, learning must have taken place, because at one time the young infant had no such ability, later it did; something must have happened during this period and what can this be if it is not learning? Of course something must have happened. Has the child learned how to raise its arm? This question surely invites the illegitimate 'How then does it do it?' Or, is it that saying that learning has occurred is simply another way of saying that it has acquired the ability to raise its arm? This, however, cannot be the substance of the contention (if it were, there might be no objection to *giving* the term 'learning' this anaemic use provided that one were perfectly clear that one were doing so) since the appeal to learning has been made in order to explain the change: the child now has, whereas before it did not have, the ability to raise its arm *because* it has learned. Is it that the child is at first guided in some way when it begins to raise its arm at will? In that case we should ask, 'By what is it guided?'; and here we are threatened by all of the muddles that surround the term 'kinaesthetic sensations'. Or is it that the young infant carefully observes the motion of its arm and guides its movement by closely observing its rise, just as a skilled batsman may alter the precise swing of his bat by attending to the curving flight of the approaching ball? But in that case, how does the infant get its arm to rise? Does it discover its arm rising and then adjust its movement? In any case, the infant, if it 'learns' to raise its arm at will, 'learns' to do so without observation of any sort, without being guided in any way at all; that is to say, once it is able to raise its arm at will it is able to do so without observation of its rise and without being guided in any way by what it sees and feels. Surely learning by being guided is far too sophisticated a performance to ascribe to the very young infant! In point of fact such performances are possible only for beings already equipped with what psychologists label 'motor-control'—only beings who already have the primitive ability to move their limbs as they please can guide their limbs by what they feel and see. Indeed, guiding one's bodily movements in this way occurs only in very special cases (*e.g.* the safecracker guided by what he feels in his finger-tips as he skilfully unlocks the safe, the person who finds the lock by feel in pitch darkness as he prepares to insert the key, and so on); normally one is not guided by anything at all as one raises one's arm.

How then shall we understand this talk about an infant's 'learning' the use of its limbs? Here, I suggest, we have a frequently unwitting and drastic modification of the everyday use of the word. If a child learns the procedure of unlocking and opening a door, it is acquiring a skill, the pre-requisite of this being the control it has over the bodily movements involved in the action it learns to perform. Here instruction is possible—the child can be taught how to acquire this skill; and whether or not it learns how to unlock and open doors by being taught to do so, the question 'How is it done?' is intelligible and answerable. Further, it makes sense in this case to ask not only why it performs the bodily movements which in fact it does perform in the operation of unlocking and opening the door (here the answer would be that it is doing these things in order to unlock and open the door), but also why it is unlocking and opening the door (it wants to get out, perhaps); but in the case of the behaviour of the very young infant before it achieves the control of its bodily movements, nothing of this sort applies. When the infant blinks as a light is flashed in its eyes, the question 'How?' is quite unlike the question 'How is it done?' which refers to a matter of human action rather than to one of mere bodily happening. To ask 'How does it blink?' is to ask 'How does the blinking occur?' which calls for an account of the mechanism involved in blinking. Similarly, 'Why does it blink?' is answered, not by stating what it is the infant wants to do or is trying to get done, but by giving some physiological account of the matter. In short, the behaviour in question is the physiological response of an organism; and if we are to speak of the actions of such a being we are employing a concept of action stripped of many of the features of our familiar concept of a human action—'action' as applied to the very young infant can be dealt with, very largely at any rate, in physiological terms. Now if the term 'learning' is to be applied to developments that ensue from *these* circumstances—in consequence of which the infant comes to attend and respond to its immediate surroundings, and in doing so begins to achieve a measure of control over the movements of its limbs— the 'learning' in question cannot be identified with the familiar learning of skills by relatively mature human beings. And in point of fact what psychologists often have in mind when they apply 'learning' to the changes that take place in the case of the very young infant is nothing more or less than the physiological development or maturation that takes place in the nervous system. Indeed, they sometimes go further and employ not only 'learning' but other related terms like 'skill', 'action', 'motive', etc., in similarly altered ways, not only with respect to very young infants but even with respect to mature human beings.[1] When this happens, psychology becomes a branch of physiology.

There is nothing intrinsically objectionable in radical alterations of the uses of terms borrowed from everyday discourse; the history of the sciences affords us many examples of this phenomenon. The trouble in the case of the psychologist's practice is that all too frequently the radical shifts in the use of such terms as 'skill', 'learning', 'action', 'motive', and so on, go unnoticed. When, therefore, the question of the relevance of his discourse is raised to the familiar matters commonly described by these terms in their everyday uses, the replies usually given are something less than satisfactory. In one breath we are sometimes told by the psychologist both that the everyday uses of these key terms are vague and obscure and that he is concerned to explain familiar psychological phenomena. This is a paradigm of logical incoherence. If the terms are obscure and vague, then what is equally obscure and vague is the scope of the subject-matter for which explanations are required. On the other hand the clarification of terms, which delimits this scope, cannot provide causal explanations of the items to which they are applied. In any case what is of central importance for our present inquiry is the confusion of subject-matters involved in this unwitting and radical alteration in the uses of crucial terms. For the 'explanations' advanced are matters of physiology—the development of the nervous system and musculature, and what such accounts purport to explain, is the fact

[1] Hence the title of a lecture recently brought to the attention of the writer: 'Physiological Motivations of Hunger'.

71

that beings endowed with such developed bodily mechanisms are capable not only of moving their limbs at will but also of performing the very many sorts of things to which we have applied the term 'human action': the unlocking and opening of doors, signalling, etc., etc. Here the crucial term is 'explanation', the meaning of which must remain obscure unless and until we have become clear about the gap, to which we referred earlier, between matters of physiological or bodily happenings and matters of human action. No doubt a comprehension of the details of the bodily mechanism will enable us to provide a causal explanation of the fact that arms and legs get moved in such-and-such ways given such-and-such excitations of the sense organs. No doubt, too, a being who lacks the developed bodily mechanism with which intelligent human beings are endowed is incapable of performing various actions including the action of raising one's arm at will. But if we distinguish, as we must, between the rising of one's arm and the action of raising one's arm it is not at all clear that if we offer a causal explanation of the former in terms of events within the bodily mechanism we are *eo ipso* offering a causal explanation of the latter. Until we can get clear about the distinction between bodily happenings (one's arm rising) and bodily action (the raising of one's arm), the relevance of discourse about the bodily mechanism to matters of human conduct must remain obscure. Indeed, it must appear problematic at best that the physiological psychologist who purports to be attempting to explain human action is addressing himself to his ostensible subject-matter.

CHAPTER EIGHT

'ACTION EQUALS BODILY MOVEMENT PLUS MOTIVE'

I SHALL now very briefly review the course of the previous argument. In Chapter III, a number of questions were raised about the relations between the events described as 'muscles in the arm moving in such-and-such ways', 'raising one's arm' and 'signalling'. We have now seen that while ordinarily the muscle-movements referred to may be said to cause the arm to rise, it is by no means clear that they function as cause of that action described as 'my raising my arm'— there is, as we have seen, a disparity between the descriptions 'one's arm rising' and 'raising one's arm', the former being a matter of bodily happening, the latter a matter of human action. Yet it is true that when, in normal circumstances, my arm rises as I signal, the rising of the arm *is* also describable as my action of raising my arm. What we can say, therefore, is that the movement of muscles causes the bodily happening which is in some sense *involved in* the action of raising the arm. We have therefore to inquire into the nature of the relation between the bodily happening and the action of raising the arm. And since, as we have seen, an instance of my arm rising cannot be identified as an instance of my raising my arm on the ground that the former is produced by certain events, mental or physical—a bodily happening cannot be construed as a bodily action by reference to the order of causes—we must now ask how it is that something described as the rising of my arm may also be described as my raising my arm. Indeed, we shall have to get clear about the relations between the descriptions 'raising my arm' and 'signalling' since, as we remarked earlier in Chapter III, raising my arm *is*, in the appropriate circumstances, signalling. In short, we need to understand more clearly the relations between the events (I use this word as a neutral term for both matters of bodily happening and matters of human action) described as 'muscle-movements of such-and-such a sort', 'arm rising', 'raising the arm' and 'signalling'. Evidently this matter is far more difficult than it appeared to be when we first considered the suggestion that just as one signals by raising one's arm, so one raises one's arm by having certain muscles move. The muscle-movements cause that bodily happening described as 'the arm rising'. But although the bodily happening needs to be distinguished from the action of raising the arm, the former, in appropriate circumstances, is the very same event as the latter. So, too, while 'raising the arm' and 'signalling' are different descriptions, a case of the former does not produce, but in appropriate circumstances is the very same thing as, a case of the latter. How is this possible?

First we need to consider more closely a suggestion mentioned in Chapter III that an action is no mere item of 'overt behaviour' but this together with something else, a motive. 'Overt behaviour', we are sometimes told, is something merely 'physical', something less than an action. The formula, then, is that action equals 'overt behaviour' plus motive. What precisely can we make of this? 'Overt behaviour' would seem to mean behaviour that is open to view, public, capable of being seen by an observer. And what can be meant by the statement that such behaviour is something merely physical? If someone signals a turn as he is driving his car, surely his action of signalling no less than the motion of his arm as it rises is normally open to view, capable of being seen by other motorists on the road. Are we to say that no one ever sees anyone else raising his arm, signalling or doing any of the very many sorts of things people do in their daily activities? Or is it that 'sees' is being used in some special technical sense so that in that special sense it is false that anyone ever sees anyone else ever doing anything at all? Or, that what we commonly speak of as seeing in such instances is not, strictly speaking, just seeing, but seeing together with something else, perhaps interpreting, inferring or what have you? The doctrine that 'overt behaviour' is something less than human action appears to be loaded with suggestions—epistemological overtones—that cry out for careful and detailed examination. Here is something merely physical: the consideration that no human being could be 150 feet tall, for this is wholly explicable in terms of the physical properties of bones, muscles and other tissues. Again, that the arm rises when such-and-such muscles move is a physical matter wholly accountable in terms of the forces exerted together with certain elementary principles of mechanics. But when one sees someone raise his arm as he signals in what sense is he seeing something merely physical? Certainly he is seeing a bodily happening—the arm rising; but he is not observing the physical process of forces applied by muscle movements to such-and-such points in the arm structure. 'Physical' would seem to be jargon for 'bodily' and suggests in any case a contrast with 'mental'. The formula then is best understood as saying that an action is a bodily movement plus an interior mental occurrence—a motive. The rising of my arm is a case of my raising my arm if and only if there is this mental occurrence of a motive.

Now it is certainly true that wherever motives can be cited there at any rate is the arena in which actions may be performed. This is not to say that if a person has a motive for doing something, he will necessarily do it; a man may have a motive for killing his wife but excellent reasons for refraining from doing so. But where motives can be cited in order to explain behaviour, there at any rate we have actions—the motives are then the motives for the actions thereby explained. The use of this preposition 'for' following the term 'motive' shows something important about the concept of a motive. And it is the use of this preposition that needs to be examined in connection with the view that an action consists of a bodily movement or happening plus some interior mental event identified as a motive. If what makes the rising of one's arm, for example, a case of the action described as 'raising one's arm' is the presence of an interior mental event called the 'motive', of what action is this alleged motive a motive? By hypothesis this motive cannot be the motive for the rising of the arm since this is only a bodily happening, and motives, whatever else they may be, are motives for actions. Can the action of which this constituent motive is the motive be the raising of the arm? This surely cannot be true; for if it were, the idea of the motive would presuppose the idea of the action to be explained. In that case the alleged explanation of the action of raising the arm is hopelessly circular. In other words: it is impossible to define the action of raising the arm in terms of a bodily movement plus motive, since the alleged motive, if it is really one, has to be understood as the motive for some action performed or performable by the agent; and if this motive is the motive for raising the arm, the motive, far from defining or constituting that action, presupposes it.

The formula under examination proposes to define 'raising one's arm', for example, in terms of the rising of one's arm together with the presence of some mental occurrence labelled a 'motive'. Let it be granted for the moment that an action can be construed as a bodily happening plus some other interior occurrence—that this will not do at all I shall attempt to show in the sequel. What the argument presented above shows is that even if one could construe an action as a bodily happening plus some other factor, that factor cannot possibly be a motive. Here the logical feature of the term 'motive', namely that a motive is the motive for an action, is of crucial importance. If the factor were a motive it must needs be the motive for an action. But of what action is this alleged motive a motive? The action cannot be the rising of the arm—that is merely a bodily happening. Can it be the action of raising the arm? If so, then the account is circular: it explains the conception of the action of raising the arm in terms of bodily happening plus motive, and then proceeds to explain the motive in terms of the very action of raising the arm for which an explanation was ostensibly given. But if the action of which the constituent motive is not the action of raising the arm, some other action must be cited, and the same difficulty breaks out once more. In short, on the present view, the expression 'motive for an action' becomes unintelligible. No doubt there is an important logical connection between motives and actions, but that connection cannot be construed as that of part to whole.

But it is a mistake in principle to attempt to define an action as a bodily happening plus any other concurrent event, mental or bodily. Let the action of raising the arm be A, the bodily occurrence B, and the concurrent event C. Then any such definition alleges that A is B plus C. Now A is an action, hence the description of A must exhibit the logical features of an action. For one thing, given that A has taken place, it follows from the account of A that someone performed it. Nothing of this sort follows from the description of B as a bodily happening. It must then follow from the description of B together with that of the interior occurrence C. But what sort of description of C can be given such that given it and the description of B, it follows that the action A has been performed? Only if a reference to the logical feature of A, as an action, is contained in the description of C, would this entailment hold. That is to say, C must be understood as that which makes such a bodily happening as the rise of one's arm a case of one's raising one's arm. But no concurrent event C distinct from B could have this logical property that it involves a logically necessary relation to any other event, specifically to event B. What alone can make the rising of my arm my action of raising my arm is that which makes it so; but that which makes it so cannot be another event distinct from the bodily event itself.

This is not to deny that we can offer descriptions of occurrences in terms of their relational, perhaps causal, properties. Certainly we very often do so. Let us then characterize C in terms of some relational property it has with respect to B and hence to A. In that case, however, I shall not know that I have performed the action A unless I am aware of the occurrence C and indeed of the bodily occurrence B. But that I am raising my arm I can vouch for no matter what goes on at the time my arm rises, whereas if A were B plus C, I could not know that a case of A occurred unless I knew that C occurred. What goes on in the way of interior events may be anything or nothing when I raise my arm. But suppose *per impossibile* that I must know that some C is taking place in order to be able to vouch for the occurrence of the action A. That C has some relational property with respect to B and hence with respect to A is after all a matter of fact that cannot be established by any inspection of C by itself. Hence even if in raising my arm I were aware of some interior occurrence C together with the bodily movement of my arm rising, it still would not follow that I could vouch for the fact that I am raising my arm. In addition, I must know that C has the required relational property. Grant, then, that A is B plus C, that in order to vouch for A I must be aware not only of C but also of the relational property that C has with respect to both B and A, what can this relational property be? If the property is a causal property, I must know then that the occurrence of C produces the occurrence of B. But unless C is something describable as my action (in which case we have moved in a full circle), nothing about any action performed is deducible from the knowledge of B and its production by another event C. And if the relational property is not a causal property, what on earth can it be? In short, the logical force of an action cannot be derived from any set of statements about happenings and their properties. The contention that my arm's rising is a case of my raising my arm because of the presence of some concurrent event simply will not do. No doubt *something* makes the rising of my arm the action of my raising my arm, but that *something* cannot be another event distinct from the mere bodily happening.

In one respect, moreover, the formula we have been considering is too strong. It asserts that the presence of a motive is a necessary condition of the occurrence of an action, but the presence of a motive is neither a necessary nor a sufficient condition. Not a sufficient condition, since a person may refrain from acting on a motive; a jealous person, aware of his jealousy, may for that very reason refrain from acting jealously— indeed he may go out of his way to benefit the person of whom he is jealous. Not a necessary condition, since a person may act without a motive. If I say, in reply to the question 'Why did you do that?', 'No reason at all; I just did', must I be lying or mistaken? Certainly a person may do something when he is well aware of what he is doing, when he is not acting from habit, on impulse or under hypnosis, and where he has no motive for what he does. Some of these cases are odd, others not. Suppose, for example, I wear a blue shirt rather than a white one; must I have a motive for putting on the blue one? I might have a motive: this one goes with my suit or my tie; but again I might have no motive at all and this sort of case is not infrequent. There are other cases in which something is amiss but in which no motive is present and the reply that can be given to the question 'Why did you do it?' is something else again. In Camus' *The Stranger* a man kills an Arab on the sun-drenched beach. He had no intention of doing so and later when asked for the motive for his crime can only reply, 'It was because of the sun.' Is that a motive? The man's remark makes no sense although in some way we can understand the whole history of the incident for all its irrationality. (Indeed, we can understand someone who tells us, 'Last night I dreamed that I bought five pounds of virtue at the flower shop', even though it is nonsensical to speak of virtue as this sort of purchaseable item.) The words are without sense, but the man and his action for all their strangeness are not altogether unintelligible; if they were we should be, as indeed we are not, appalled by his utter inhumanity. Or suppose, to consider the case posed by G. E. M. Anscombe, '... someone hunted out all the green books in his house and spread them out carefully on the roof' and when asked 'Why?' replies 'No particular reason; I just thought I would' (*Intention*, p. 26); here the words are intelligible, but not the man.

There would seem to be, therefore, various sorts of cases where things done are done without motive. And as Anscombe remarks about the general reply to the question 'Why?', namely, 'No particular reason; I just did', such answers 'are often quite intelligible; sometimes strange; and sometimes unintelligible' (*loc. cit.*). The formula that an action is a bodily movement plus a motive, all other objections aside, is too simple to fit the wide variety of cases that need to be considered—that there is a motive for every action is altogether doubtful.

Does all of this mean that there is no logical connection between motives and action? Not at all. Does it mean that where no motive is present, the action is inexplicable? Certainly not. In order to resolve these matters it will be necessary to look more carefully at the character of motives and the manner in which these explain conduct.

CHAPTER NINE

MOTIVE AND EXPLANATION

IN the preceding chapter I remarked that there is a logical connection between the concept of a motive and that of an action; a motive is a motive for some action either performed or considered; hence a motive, far from being a factor which when conjoined with any bodily movement thereby constitutes an action, actually presupposes the very concept of an action itself. Indeed, if the argument in the preceding chapter is sound, it is impossible to account for the logical features of an action by any alchemical process of conjoining bodily movements with any concurrent events, mental or physical. It remains therefore to exhibit the logical connection between motives and action and in order to do this it is necessary that we look more closely at the character of motives.

Now the term 'motive' applies not only to emotions (*e.g.* of rage, jealousy, etc.) but also to intentions. In order to simplify the discussion, I shall restrict the application of the term 'motive', in this chapter, to the case of intentions.

It is a familiar view, suggested by the etymology of the term, that a motive is some occurrence that functions as a spring to action. A motive moves; a man's motives are the things that motivate him, cause him to do, provide the inner pushes that issue in action. The sequence 'motive—action' is thus pictured as a peculiar mechanical relation that bridges the gap between the mental and the bodily. Nevertheless, it is no matter of etymology that nourishes and sustains the hold upon our imagination of this picture of the proceedings. After all, *but for, did he not have, in the absence of* (other familiar locutions come to mind) the motives a person does in fact have, his conduct would not be what in fact it is. And if the question is raised whether or not it was John Smith who brutally assaulted Edward Jones, the matter of motives is surely relevant. John Smith *could not* have done this foul deed unless he was moved to do so by . . . (here the account is to be completed by describing a motive requisite for the deed). This sort of consideration, and no mere matter of etymology, gives almost compelling force to the notion that motives are quasi-mechanical causes of something labelled 'overt behaviour', that they are items that explain what a person does in the sense in which events are explained by reference to their causes.

Yet this picture of the proceedings is certainly defective. Let a motive be a cause in anything like the Humean sense of this term: some interior mental event. Then the effect is another event. Suppose, to return to our example, I am signalling by raising my arm. One thing that happens (and this *will* fit the Humean model of an effect) is that my arm rises. Let the causal sequence, then, be as follows: motive → bodily movement. But this will not do. By hypothesis a motive explains an *action* ('But for his motive, *he would not have done* such-and-such'). If the causal

84

sequence is motive→bodily movement, no action is being explained at all. In order to provide the envisaged causal explanation of the action, the bodily movement has to be further identified as the bodily movement that occurs when the action is performed. Hence in order to explain the action, for example, of my raising my arm, by citing the motive as a Humean cause of the bodily movement that consists in the rising of my arm, it is necessary to conjoin the statement of the causal relation (motive→bodily movement) with a further statement connecting the bodily movement with the action to be explained. But this latter statement, that the rising of my arm occurs when I raise my arm, is not itself a statement of a fact of Humean causality—bodily movements do not *produce* nor are they produced by the actions in which they are involved; for it is the very same thing that is the rising of my arm that is also describable as my raising my arm. Are these alternative descriptions of the same events ('my arm rising', 'my raising of my arm') alternative ways of saying the same thing? Certainly not. Are they alternative descriptions of the same event in the way in which 'arm rising' and 'fingers unclasping' describe the same bodily movement? Once more the answer must be No! No further description of the bodily movement in respect of its properties as a bodily movement could possibly disclose that additional feature that makes it a case of an action. If, then, we start with the motive as an interior event that functions as a cause of the bodily movement, no explanation in Humean causal terms of the action is possible.

Let us set aside, for the moment, the problem of

bridging the gap between bodily movements and actions. Let us even suppose, for the moment, that the motive is an event that stands in a causal relation to the action. Can this be the sense in which a motive explains the action? Is the 'but for', 'in the absence of', etc., when these locutions are applied to actions, the 'but for', the 'in the absence of', etc., that figure in such statements as, 'But for (in the absence of, etc.) the high concentration of petrol vapour in the air, the explosion would not have occurred'?

Consider someone raising his arm as he drives his car towards an intersection. Ordinarily the question, 'Why did he raise his arm?' would not be asked, not because it is senseless but because there would be no point to asking it—we know what is going on and hence know the answer to the question. But someone unfamiliar with what is happening might ask the question and here the answer might be given that he raised his arm in order to indicate to others that he was preparing to make a turn. This is a case of citing a motive—the driver's reason for doing what he did. Now the supposition that this motive is an interior mental event that could stand in Humean causal relations to anything else, in particular to the action of raising the arm, is exposed to the following simple empirical objection: when the driver raised his arm, what mental occurrence did in fact take place? Suppose that at the time of the action all that crossed his mind was 'Another god-awful turn in this anti-quated road!', would that have falsified the answer to the question 'Why?'? And if one is still strongly tempted to say that there must have been something in his mind identifiable as his motive for his doing what he did, why the *must*? Here Wittgenstein's familiar admonition, 'Don't think, look', is appropriate. That his motive was such and such, that something crossed his mind, these surely are matters of fact. And if the driver himself is unable to find the mental occurrence, is this due to the fact that it is elusive, that it escapes him?[1] He intended to make the turn—this is why he raised his arm—he raised his arm in order to indicate to others that he was preparing to make a turn. But does the 'in order to indicate that . . .' mark some mental occurrence? Nevertheless we can say that the following did in fact happen: the driver indicated his intention to prepare to make a turn. His indicating that he was about to make a turn is something that happened. This, surely, is different from merely raising his arm, and what can the difference consist in except this, that something was going on at the time, some event that was his motive? Let us then suppose that *something* went on, an event that is common and peculiar to all such cases. Let us suppose, further, that this elusive something is the motive, the cause of the driver's raising his arm. And, to repeat, let us ignore the consideration that this cause would seem to have as its effect the bodily movement, rather than the action of raising the arm. I shall argue that this supposition is logically incoherent.

In any simple causal explanation of one event by reference to another, it is not the identity or the character of the effect that is at issue, but the condi-

---

[1] 'Here it is easy to get into that dead-end in philosophy, where one believes that the difficulty of the task consists in this: our having to describe phenomena that are hard to get hold of, the present experience that slips quickly by, or something of the kind.' L. Wittgenstein, *Philosophical Investigations*, p. 129e.

tions in which it occurs—how it came to be. Antecedently of the causal explanation given, we know quite well what the event thereby explained is. A causal explanation, in other words, does not give us a further characterization of the event thereby explained (except of course in the trivial sense that it characterizes it as an event that has a certain cause); rather, it offers us an account of how it is that an event whose characteristics are already known is brought to pass. Now on the present supposition, the motive for the action of raising the arm is an event that causes that action to take place. The motive, however, is the motive for the action. Hence, on this supposition, the motive for the action is the cause of the action. This, however, is self-contradictory. As the alleged cause of the action, it cannot serve further to characterize the action. As motive it must—for it tells us what in fact the person was doing. It informs us, *qua* motive, that the action of raising the arm was in fact the action of giving information to others to the effect that the driver was preparing to make a turn. Now this, leaving aside the fact that signalling is a conventionalized method of doing this, is in effect to make it clear that the action of raising the arm was indeed the action of signalling. In short, citing the motive was giving a fuller characterization of the action; it was indeed providing a better understanding of what the driver was doing. But no Humean cause could possibly do this; any alleged cause, in this sense, of the action of raising the arm (here we may waive the difference between the rising of the arm and the action of raising the arm) would merely explain how the action of raising the arm came to be. From the

88

driver's statement that he raised his arm in order to inform others of what he was about to do, it follows logically that he was signalling or at least attempting to signal. If, then, the motive were some event either concurrent with or antecedent to the action of raising the arm, there would needs be a logically necessary connection between two distinct events—the alleged motive and the action, however it is described. This is impossible if the sequence motive→action is a causal relation. It is equally impossible if the motive is some interior mental event distinct from that event that is the action of raising the arm. Hence, if the motive explains what was done, the explanation is not and cannot be the type of explanation exhibited in the explanation of natural phenomena, whether these be the excitation of muscles, the movements of limbs, the explosion of petrol vapours or the behaviour of falling bodies.

This result should not be surprising. In our discussion in Chapter V of Prichard's predicament in respect of the notion of an act of volition, it will be recalled that such acts were held by him to exhibit two distinct features: they were alleged to function as causes of the ensuing actions and, it was conceded, they could not be described except by reference to these very actions. These requirements, as we saw, are self-contradictory; and Prichard's predicament comes down to this, that he was unable to resist accepting both of these logically incompatible features of the alleged acts of volition. But hopeless as his conclusions may be, there was sound instinct in Prichard's insistence that an act of volition must be described by reference to the relevant action, not merely because the alternative thereby avoided was a hopeless multiplication of indefinables but more importantly because of the appreciation, muddied and obscured as it was, of the relevant concept of explanation that is familiarly applied to human conduct. If we are to explain a person's action, *e.g.* his raising his arm, by reference to an act of volition in anything like the sense in which one explains this action by citing a motive (he indicates that he is about to make a turn), the description of the alleged volition must make it clear *what* action is being performed. In other words, it must be so described that, given this description together with the statement that the action of raising the arm is taking place, it follows logically that what the person is doing is signalling. This is how citing a motive makes it clear what the action being performed is. The incoherence involved in the doctrine of acts of volition is the confounding of two quite distinct senses of 'explanation': causal explanation with the familiar explanation of conduct in terms of motives. To the extent to which Humean causes of anything taking place when a person acts are cited, no action is being explained in this familiar and important sense. To the extent to which an action is being explained in this same sense of the term, no reference to an interior mental occurrence is being made. Since a motive, in explaining an action, makes it clear *what* the action in question is, any description or account of the motive must of necessity involve a reference to an action being performed, and specifically to the kind of action that is thereby specified by the explanation given. Thus it is that in the case of the raising of the arm, the statement that declares the agent's motive refers, not to something that crosses the agent's mind at that moment or to any other interior occurrence, but to a matter of public performance. To say, in response to the question 'Why did you raise your arm?', 'I did so, in order to indicate that I was preparing to make a turn,' is to call attention, not to some mental occurrence, but to the action that was performed and the circumstances in which this occurred—that one was driving, that one was preparing to turn, that there were others on the road to be apprised of what it was that one was about to do—and thereby to make it clear what was going on in the public arena of human action, rather than in the hidden recesses of one's mind.

Raising one's arm and thereby signalling is a highly conventionalized method of communication. This means, first, that there are fixed rules of the road that determine the precise form in which the relevant bodily movement is to be executed. Second, it involves the convention that whenever this bodily movement occurs in the appropriate circumstances, then, whatever the agent's intentions may be, the movement of one's arm will be understood as an instance of signalling. If, for example, there is a doubt in the minds of other drivers on the road who observe the extended arm, the doubt is not as to whether the person who extended his arm is signalling, but rather as to whether he is doing this inadvertently—not mindful of the circumstances he might, for example, be pointing to something of interest during his conversation with his passenger. In such cases one signals, whether or not one intended to do so and equally of course whatever one's motive may have been—the circumstances and the rules of the road are decisive here, just as a chess player, who may not intend to move his piece, has committed himself to doing so when he adjusts it without uttering the conventional excusing formula. In cases of this sort, the conventions, rather than the agent's intentions, determine what is being done. 'I didn't mean to do that' does not controvert the claim that the action was performed; admitting inattention, it serves as a defence against some other and perhaps more serious charge—stupidity, wilfulness, and so on.

Now it might be thought that in arguing as I have that the motive of one's raising one's arm, when one signals, is not to be identified with any mental occurrence—that anything in fact might have crossed the agent's mind at that time—I have traded on this highly conventionalized feature of the action of signalling. Suppose, however, that the action of signalling is intentional, surely something relevant to one's intention in raising one's arm does cross one's mind: one attends to what it is that one is doing, recognizes that the turn is ahead, observes, perhaps, that a car is following closely behind and wants the driver to slow down in order to avoid a collision as one slows down for the turn. Surely, it will be objected, these items pass through one's mind, and are these not relevant to the intention or motive one has in raising one's arm, namely, to indicate what one is about to do?

Certainly they are relevant. The action cited is a full-blooded example of an intentional action, one done not through habit, inadvertence, impulse, absent-mindedness or, as it might have occurred in other circumstances, for no reason at all. The agent was careful, cautious and considerate; in Descartes' omnibus sense of the term, thinking was going on, in a pattern that explains what the agent was doing in raising his arm.

Nevertheless, there are cautions to be observed. I have contended not only that the intention cannot function as a Humean cause of the action of raising the arm, on the ground that if it did it could not possibly explain the action in the sense in which actions are explained by intentions, but also that the intention cannot be identified with any of the items that cross the agent's mind during the incident. To begin with, even in the example noted above—a full-blown case of an intentional action in which the person is careful, cautious, considerate and observant—where in the history of the incident is that factor labelled 'the intention'? Is it the thought, 'There is the turn ahead!'? But this thought can be an idle thought, something that strikes me, a passenger, as I too watch the road. If the thought is to be relevant to the deed, the driver must do something about it. As a passenger, I too may have the thought—can it then be said that I have a motive for raising my arm? That would be an idle gesture on my part—if I had the thought and raised my arm, would that be doing what the driver does when he raises his arm? It cannot be the mere thought, then, that is the driver's intention or motive. Is it then the driver's wanting to do something about the thought? But what does he want to do? If he were asked when he raises his arm, 'Why are you doing that?', he might say, 'Because I want to turn at the intersection.' Is, then, the intention he has in raising his arm, wanting to make the turn? But equally well he might have replied, 'Because I want to stop at the

93

grocer's' and even 'Because I want to be sure I have food in the house for supper tonight.' However, these replies inform us of the intention of the driver in signalling. The 'that' in the question, 'Why are you doing that?', will have been taken to refer, if the answers given are satisfactory, not to the mere raising of the arm, but to this action understood as a case of signalling a turn. What we want to discover is that factor in the things that crowd in upon the driver's reflections that can be identified as the intention that makes the raising of the arm a case of signalling a turn. Shall we then say that what makes the former a case of the latter is this, that the driver wants to raise his arm? But a driver does not want to raise his arm, he just does it. Normally we do not want to move our limbs, nor do we try to do so. Normally there is nothing that can possibly go awry: there are no cautions to be observed, no calculations to be made, no procedure to adopt which might fail to get us what it is that we want—we simply move our limbs. Besides, even if in raising his arm, the driver wanted to do so, his answer to the question, 'Why did you raise your arm?', 'Because I wanted to,' would be no answer at all, but a rude rebuff. Where then in the things that come to the mind of the driver is the intention with which he raises his arm? Is it the thought that he is indicating to others that he is preparing to make a turn? But must he say to himself, 'Now I am preparing to make a turn'? Grant that he is careful, cautious, considerate, fully aware of what he is doing and of what is going on —he might of course say this to himself, but he need not. Someone exceedingly deliberate in his actions, *e.g.* someone learning to drive, might go through this mental step; but this is not typical of the general run of cases. The driver has learned to do what he does, without reflecting on it. Ordinarily, he simply takes note of what is going on about him—the traffic and the approaching intersection—and raises his arm. Suppose, however, that the driver actually says to himself, 'Now I am about to make a turn' and does so. If later he remembers that he was about to make a turn at that time—this is why he raised his arm—what must he remember? That he said this to himself? But he might have said this to himself without meaning it. What then did he remember when he remembered himself meaning it? Here Wittgenstein remarks about the familiar reply that meaning it must have been some sort of inner experience, 'And now remember *quite precisely*! Then the "inner experience" of intending seems to vanish again. Instead one remembers thoughts, feelings, movements and also connections with earlier situations' (*Philosophical Investigations*, §645).

But suppose in fact that what one remembers is some particular feeling or experience, something that always happens when one intends to indicate that one is preparing to make a turn, when one raises one's arm, would *that* be the intention? So if when I sit wrapped in silence beside the driver and this feeling comes to me as I raise my arm, am I also intending to signal? It would be a curious accident, calling for some sort of psychological explanation, if certain experiences were had in all those cases and in only those cases in which by raising one's arm one signalled. The oddity of this case, the fact that it would call for a psychological explanation, implies that the intention must not be identified with such experiences.

What the driver sees, feels and thinks, when he raises his arm to indicate a turn will depend upon a great many varied circumstances—the particular conditions of the traffic on the road, the special features of the road and its surroundings, his state of mind at the time, his interests, mood, purposes, and so on. The search for a central nuclear experience that is the intention blinds us to the very complex and enormously varied experiences that surround the performances of this relatively simple sort of action; this together with a tendency to employ stereotypes in our thinking about cases of this sort, to restrict our attention to some special case, the special features of which are then taken as paradigmatic of all of the cases to which we should attend, induces a sophistication that clouds and obscures our view of the details of our experience.[1] In this matter we need to be more, not less, ingenuous in order not to miss what lies open to view.

Now some of the things one thinks and feels and does at the time are relevant, some not, to the incident of raising one's arm in order to signal. One is driving on the road, one has learned the rules of the road, one sees an approaching turn, one notices a car following closely behind, one sees a garage on the corner; one feels relief (At long last, home is just around the corner!) or irritation (Another turn, another minute late!), a tension as one braces for a quick deceleration

[1] 'A main cause of philosophical disease—a one-sided diet: one nourishes one's thinking with only one kind of example.' *Philosophical Investigations*, §593.

or a relaxing of the muscles of the leg as one moves it from the strained position at the accelerator; the list of such items could be multiplied indefinitely. Some of these are relevant to any intentional action of signalling (the agent is driving a car, he has learned to manipulate it, and in doing so to follow rules of the road including the one that requires him to raise his arm in order to indicate a turn, he sees a turn approaching, etc.); some are relevant to the special features of a given situation (the anxiety felt because of the car following much too closely, the relief at the sight of the turn that means home and its comforts after a very exhausting trip); some would seem to be irrelevant to this or virtually any other instance of signalling (the sight of the clouds in the sky, or the itch at the tip of his nose); some are irrelevant to the given instances of signalling but would be relevant were the circumstances altered appropriately (one's annoyance, that might have been occasioned by the serious delay resulting from having to turn into a dirt road, but which is now occasioned by the silly prattle from one's passenger). Similar considerations apply to the actions of the driver at the wheel, the movements of arms and legs, the turn of the head, the blink of the eyes, the slight movements of the body. These things and many others occur in indefinitely varied ways before, during, and after the action of raising the arm in order to indicate a turn.

Where then is the intention with which the driver raises his arm? Certainly no single occurrence can be identified as the intention. Is it then a feature of the raising of the arm that makes it intentional? But someone observing the driver raising his arm and asking, 'Why does he do it?' may have a clear view of the movement of his arm. Indeed, if he thought that by looking closely at this bodily action, he would discover the intention, this would establish that he simply did not understand the word 'intention'. Signalling is not a feature or style of the bodily action of raising the arm in the way in which bringing it to a horizontal or to a vertical position is. Nor is it quite correct to say that the intention is that which is aimed at—the objective. It is of course true that what follows the action of raising the arm is relevant to the intention. The very account of the intention—to indicate that one is about to make a turn—involves a reference to the future. One can change one's mind, decide not to do what one indicated one was about to do; but changing one's mind is intelligible only by reference to what one is of a mind to do. In other words, it would be logically impossible to explain the intention one had in raising one's arm except by reference to some future proceedings in which one engaged or would be expected to engage. But the reference to the future does not exhaust the logically important features of the intention. It might be equally important, indeed, in explaining the intention to someone, to refer to what had happened—to what had been brought to pass. 'Why is he raising his arm?' 'See, he has been driving and has arrived at our intersection.' This too might well serve to explain matters, to fill in details and thus to make clear the intention. Earlier I remarked that in stating his intention in raising his arm, the person is explaining what he is doing. But what he is doing has to be understood as referring not to a present moment, sliced off so to speak from what has gone before and what will follow, but to the present action as an incident in the total proceedings: the driver is on the road, has arrived at an intersection, is about to turn, and is indicating that he is preparing to do so. In declaring his intention in raising his arm, the driver is explaining what he is doing and he is explaining what he is doing, *i.e.* that he is signalling, by directing attention to the context in which the raising of his arm is understood as signalling.

But these circumstances, it will be objected, do not establish that the signalling was intentional. The driver may have arrived at the intersection, he may be preparing to turn, and he may in fact do so; but he may be raising his arm in order to point to something of interest to his passenger and hence not signal intentionally. Must he not know what he is doing when he signals intentionally, and is not what he thus knows his intention? Certainly he must know what he is doing, but knowing what he is doing is taking due account of what is happening about him in acting as he does at the wheel including giving the proper signal. And certainly he knows what he is about to do and that what he is doing when he is raising his arm is giving the required signal. But what passes through his mind will once more depend upon a wide variety of possible factors including his further intention in giving the signal (to turn into the approaching intersection, and doing this in order that . . .); and these factors which impinge upon what crosses his mind will vary from case to case. At the very moment he raises his arm in order to give the signal of an imminent turn all that may happen is that he recognizes the approaching intersection with an 'Ah, there it is!'; but what is important is the history of the incident in which actions, experiences, feelings, desires, expectations and further intentions are woven into an intelligible pattern. Hence Wittgenstein's well-known remark. ' "I am not ashamed of what I did then, but of the intention which I had"—and didn't what I did *include* the intention? What justifies the shame? The whole history of the incident' (*Philosophical Investigations*, §644).

Hence there are ways of determining whether in raising his arm, the driver's intention is to indicate a turn, to point to something of interest to his passenger, to attract the attention of a policeman who might rescue him from the kidnapper sitting at his side, to demonstrate how a signal is given (he is a driving school instructor and he and his pupil are seated in a stationary car), or to engage in a mock-performance. And there are ways of checking the correctness of declarations of intention in terms of the circumstances in which the driver is placed, his further avowals and disavowals, his further actions, the feelings he betrays, the interests he exhibits, etc.[1] These serve as checks upon the truthfulness of his declarations of intention precisely because of the fact that having an intention is a matter that pertains not to one and only one incident of the proceedings but to the whole character of the proceedings that surround the action performed. By declaring truthfully his intention or motive in raising his arm, our driver explains what he is doing by focusing our attention upon

[1] For a further account of such checks upon truthfulness see G. E. M. Anscombe's discussion in *Intention*, §25.

certain of the factors that surround the action of raising his arm. In the context of these factors, that action *is* indicating that he is about to make a turn. Given an understanding of the driver's further intentions, his interests, habits and state of mind, we should have a better grasp of the proceedings as a whole and a better understanding of the pattern of his thoughts, feelings and actions. It is not surprising, then, that in general the more we know about a man and the circumstances in which he is placed, the more assured we are about the character of his intentions in what he is doing and the better we understand his actions.

What is it then that one explains when one states one's intention in doing something, in our example, raising one's arm? One thing one does in thereby explaining one's action is to make clear what it is that one is doing. To state one's intention in raising one's arm is to declare that one is signalling. But in addition, as it should now be apparent, it is in an important sense to explain oneself, to say something about oneself. Instead of asking, 'Why are you raising your arm?', one might, when quite well aware of the fact that the person is raising his arm, ask, 'What are you doing?' And fathers, having had intelligence of the untoward and apparently wayward behaviour of their sons, do sometimes challenge them to account for their conduct no less by an 'Explain yourself!' than by a demanding 'Why did you do it?' Certainly someone asking a driver why it is that he is raising his arm, when in point of fact he is doing so in order to signal, needs to be reminded or informed of the status of the agent as someone driving on the road and bound and guided in his actions by the relevant rules of the road.[1]

How then does citing a motive explain an action? Certainly, with respect to the instance we have been discussing, stating the motive is not offering a (Humean) causal explanation of the action. The explanation does not refer us to some other event—the motive—which explains causally how the action came to be. If it did, the description of the action would remain unimpaired—we should in that case have no better description of the action itself but only a better idea of how this action, whose description remains unchanged, came to be. But as we have seen, the explanation of the action given by the statement of the motive or intention explains in a two-fold way: first, it provides us with a better understanding of the action itself by placing it with its appropriate context; and, second, it reveals something about the agent himself. By doing both of these things, the statement of motive or intention enables us to make sense of what was going on—it reveals an order or pattern in the proceedings which had not been apparent to the person who asked, 'Why are you . . .?' The person asking such a question is not looking for Humean causal explanations of what is taking place. Nor need his view of the action be obscured. He does see the

[1] 'Why do I want to tell him about an intention too, as well as telling him what I did?—Not because the intention was also going on at that time. But because I want to tell him something about *myself*, which goes beyond what happened at that time. I reveal to him something about myself when I tell him what I was going to do.' L. Wittgenstein, *Philosophical Investigations*, §659. This remark applies equally well to our example, for in explaining what I am doing when I raise my arm to signal, I am making it clear what I am about to do.

102

driver raise his arm; but whether the driver is signalling, pointing to something of interest to his passenger, attracting attention, demonstrating how to signal, the questioner is unable to tell. It is as if he were confronted with a few scattered fragments of sounds and could not discover the melodic structure of the notes he heard. Here we need to put ourselves in the position of an ingenuous or puzzled observer who is confronted with a confused welter of events that surround the action—to declare one's motive or intention to such a person is to enable him to discern the order in an apparent chaos of events and thereby to provide him with a better understanding of both the agent and the action (cf. G. E. M. Anscombe, *op. cit.*, §43).

The 'but for', 'in the absence of' in the example of a man raising his arm in order to signal—but for (in the absence of) his motive or intention, he would not have raised his arm—is therefore not the 'but for' or 'in the absence of' that marks a causally necessary condition of an event (but for the petrol vapours in the air, the explosion would not have occurred); on the contrary, it marks the whole character of the incident in which this action occurred. Our driver *might* have raised his arm for no reason at all; it would be too strong a condition to lay down that whenever someone moves his limbs he has a motive for doing so. 'He just did it' may be the only correct answer that one can give to the question 'Why?' But in other cases such an answer would be unintelligible. We should not understand at all the case in which someone, *for no reason at all*, goes through the elaborate procedure of laying flowers on every grave in a given cemetery, not because 'for no reason at all' is a senseless combination of words, but rather because we would not understand such a person. To say of such a person that he is mad is to write off the action as unintelligible. For here there is no background of reflections, interests and actions against which this elaborate action can be understood; since he is not even doing it out of sympathy, for effect or for amusement, we can only gape and write off both the man and his action as unintelligible. But in the case of our driver who raises his arm there is a background against which both the man and his action can be understood. To say 'But for his intention, he would not have raised his arm' is to reject the possibility that he did it for no reason at all. It is, in other words, to invite attention to the context of circumstances. And it is to claim that both agent and action are intelligible, the latter in a way that enables us *further* to characterize it, in our example, as the action of signalling. The last point is important. For someone might object that on this account our 'but for' statement reduces to the triviality that 'But for the intention our driver has of indicating that he was about to make a turn, he would not have indicated that he was about to make a turn,' *i.e.* 'But for the fact that he signalled, he would not have signalled.' This would be a mistake. Our 'but for' statement refers to the action as 'the action of raising the arm'; it asserts that this action, so described, was done for a reason and, since it specifies the motive, it enables those of us who are aware of the conventions of the road to characterize this very same action as 'signalling'. As such our statement is far from trivial.

CHAPTER TEN

WANTING AND WANTING TO DO

I HAVE argued that the causal model of explanation employed in the natural sciences will not fit the
very simple instance in which the motive a person has
for raising his arm—namely, in order to indicate that
he is about to make a turn—explains that action. In
arguing that such a motive or intention is not a
Humean cause[1] I have not dwelt upon the distinction
between the action of raising the arm and the bodily
movement of the arm rising; that distinction alone
should cast doubt upon the idea that the relation
between motive and action is that of cause and effect.
Nevertheless this causal picture, despite the evident
fact that it does violence to the concepts of action and
motive, does have a powerful hold upon our imaginations. One might attempt to weaken the persuasiveness of this picture or model of the proceedings by
proposing a simple alternative. Something, in fact,

[1] For purposes of my argument it matters not whether or no we
accept as adequate Hume's account of causation in the natural
sciences—all that is important here is the recognition insisted upon
by Hume that natural events (*e.g.* explosions, cell divisions, etc.)
which are causally related are logically independent of one another.
Hence the otherwise objectionable looseness with which I speak
either of a Humean cause or of a cause in the sense in which this term
is employed in the natural sciences.

could be said in favour of the application of aesthetic categories to the sense in which a motive explains an action. Our common ways of speaking do on occasion suggest such a model, just as they suggest the causal model. 'What made him (caused him to) do it?' invites a statement of motive or intention. But it is also true that we speak of an action as fitting the person, his character and his motives. 'That would be his style, his way of doing things' can be as much an imputation of motive as 'That made him do it'. We talk sometimes about the rhyme and reason of a man's behaviour no less than about the things that caused him to act in the way he did. Yet such counter-measures are indecisive. They may or may not be accidents of our ordinary ways of speaking that throw no light upon the crucial concepts that interest us. In any case the most effective and decisive way of removing the persuasiveness of the familiar causal model is to explore further and more closely the concepts with which we are concerned and by removing misconceptions break the hold this model has upon our imagination.

Here it is that we need to look more closely at a number of concepts which are closely related to those of motive and action, and which seem on the face of the matter to lend themselves to the Humean model of explanation. The most important of these is that of wanting or desiring. Certainly we can and often do explain a person's conduct by citing his desires or wants. Indeed we sometimes explain his desires in terms of his motives and intentions. And certainly we can date our desires or wants. 'At such-and-such a time I wanted such-and-such.' And I might want or desire something without betraying that fact. Surely, our wants or desires are events, and mental to boot. And since they play an important rôle in conduct it is difficult to resist the conclusion that insofar as they do so, the causal model of explanation employed in the natural sciences is in fact applicable to our everyday conduct. Here, it would seem, we have mental causal conditions of the behaviour that is open to public view.

The concept of desire plays a crucial rôle in many discussions in philosophical psychology, in moral philosophy and in so-called value theory. Paradoxically, however, it remains a much neglected topic of inquiry. It is not surprising, therefore, that the subject is surrounded with obscurity.

It would be impossible in this inquiry to examine needs or the so-called unconscious desires. Nor shall I attempt to examine the various kinds of cases describable as 'not knowing what one wants'. For sometimes this description is applied to someone who is at loose ends without quite knowing why, discontented or dissatisfied with his condition but unaware either of what is amiss or of what would remedy matters. Sometimes it is applied to the case of a person who desires something, *e.g.* a car, but has not made up his mind about the particulars of make, model, price, etc. Sometimes it is applied to the case of a person who wants something described in a general way but does not know which of various things so described would do for the particular purpose to which he wishes to put it; for example, he wants a saw in order to rip a plank but does not know whether *this* one will do rather than *that* one. Nor shall I attempt to deal with the locution 'What one *really* wants' which is used to mark, not what in fact a person desires but, rather, what would satisfy him, a matter about which, again, one can be mistaken. Again, I shall not deal with the borderline cases of desire that shade off into idle wish, for there is no clear line of division that separates these. And I shall not attempt to deal with an even more extreme case in which one says honestly that one wants such-and-such, where the description given is self-contradictory; *e.g.* someone might want to find a real number satisfying the description $\sqrt{-32}$. Rather, I shall confine my remarks to clear-cut central cases of desire properly so-called, not to cases that deviate from these in various sorts of ways. For it is only by learning to apply the term 'desire' to such standard cases that one can, first, learn how to use this term and, second, deal as one must with the various borderline cases. And whether or not the person in getting what he wants is satisfied, whether or not his needs are fulfilled, and whether or not his purposes or objectives are furthered, are issues not to be confused with the fact that he wants, as indeed he does, the particular thing he has in mind.

The familiar view is, in Hume's terminology, that a desire is an impression of reflection, an internal mental occurrence. Now the properties commonly ascribed to this occurrence are rather curious. In the first place it functions as a cause, usually sparking in some way an item of so-called overt behaviour; and when it does not do it this fact is put down to the presence of interfering causal conditions. But in addition, since a desire is a desire for something, this occurrence is held to be directed in some way at an object or event, the obtainment of which is the 'satisfaction' of the desire even though, of course, the person himself may remain dissatisfied. Commonly it is held that enjoyments and discomforts are somehow connected with desires and their satisfactions; but just <u>now</u> this is the case seems to be a matter on which there is a diversity of opinion. Hobbes, for example, identifies the desire with a movement in the body towards the object of desire, and speaks of the 'sense' or 'appearance' of this movement as a 'delight or trouble of mind' (*Leviathan*, Ch. 6). In other writers the desire itself seems to be identified with an uneasiness of the mind or some sort of tension. In still others, the desire is thought to produce an uneasiness. These are matters which involve their own peculiar difficulties and obscurities; they need not detain us here. What is important for our purpose is the prevalent idea that a desire or want is some sort of cause that is somehow directed at an object—that which is desired. I want to show that this is a muddle, that as cause it cannot be 'directed' in the relevant sense, indeed that no internal impression could possibly exhibit the logical features of a desire.

That any desire has an object, to use the familiar formula, is a logically necessary and no mere accidental feature of the desire. (This does not mean that there must *be* the thing desired, for of course I can want something that does not exist, *e.g.* one more child. Neither does this imply that it is only *things* that we want; for I also want to do certain actions. With suitable changes the following argument applies not only to 'wanting things' but also to 'wanting to do'. I deal with the former only in order to simplify the exposition of the argument.) If I say, 'Nothing',

109

in reply to the question, 'What do you desire?', I am not saying that I have a desire that is not a desire for anything at all; on the contrary, I am denying that I have any desire that is of particular relevance to the given context. A desire is a desire for something. So much so that Hobbes, interestingly enough, remarks that the various passions, including desires, 'have their names for diverse considerations diversified' among these being 'the object loved or hated' (*loc. cit.*). For if one is to give an account of any desire, nothing will do that at the very least does not make clear the kind of thing desired. But precisely how can an internal impression, some sort of inner itch, twitch or tension, exhibit this property? How can it be directed at anything at all?

Here someone might suggest the following: Since a desire when satisfied no longer operates, *e.g.* a desire for food disappears when food is obtained, to say that this internal occurrence is a desire for food is to say that the obtainment of food will dissipate it. On this suggestion, a categorical statement of the form 'A desires y' is reconstructed as a mixed categorical and hypothetical statement about inner itches or twitches, *i.e.* a statement about the circumstances in which such events, now occurring, would cease. This, of course, is a familiar type of philosophical translation; and, as in the case of phenomenalism, it should be remarked that it must be considered unhelpful as long as the notion of contrary-to-fact conditionals remains obscure. In any case there are fatal difficulties involved in this account of desires. How can I tell, on this view, what it is that I want? Not by inspecting the desire itself—the internal impression, tension, uneasiness, itch or twitch—for to know that I desire y is to have some mental occurrence x such that y would dissipate it; and this involves having causal knowledge that can only be grounded on past experiences of having had y dissipate x. This implies that the first time I desired caviar, I should have absolutely no reason to suppose that it was caviar rather than cheese that I wanted. For all that I can tell on the basis of the impression or itch of desire itself, it might well be the case that cheese or even raw kidneys, rather than caviar, would dissipate the particular impression I feel. And the account implies that it would be utterly impossible for a child to say in good faith that it wanted the moon that appeared above the foot of its bed, no matter how often it was struck by the sight. What alone would justify the child's remark, 'I want the moon', is getting it and finding that getting the moon would relieve its itch of desire. What indeed would it mean to say that anyone wants the impossible, on this account of the matter? We should never have any reason for saying that we wanted anything unless there had been occasions in which we got what we wanted. And we should have no reason whatsoever for saying that anyone wanted the impossible unless there were occasions when he got the sort of thing he wanted—the impossible! For if he really wanted the impossible, this and only this would remove the itch or twitch of desire—that is to say, nothing would remove the feeling and hence on the present account nothing was wanted at all!

Is it, however, that the child when it wants the moon has the idea of the moon and in this way knows what it wants? The trouble with this suggestion is two-fold: Setting aside the special difficulty about the impossibility of getting what it wants, can it tell from the thought that the thing thought about has the relevant causal property? And, further, there are other thoughts at the time. It is offered the toy by its placating parent and how does the child connect the itch of desire with the thought of the moon rather than with the thought of the toy? And when I want the caviar rather than the cheese, how is the thought of the caviar rather than the thought of the cheese connected with the particular tension, uneasiness (call it what you will) that I feel? Is it that I *make* the connection? How? By focusing my attention upon the impression and the thought of the caviar? But I cannot help attending to the unwanted putrescent cheese before me. And suppose that I want two distinct things—caviar and wine—is it that there are two impressions or tensions, one that hooks on to the thought of the caviar, the other to the thought of the wine? If so I might get impressions and thoughts connected together in the wrong way. Still, this will make no practical difference if I want both caviar and wine; but suppose I want only one, what is there to prevent me from connecting the tension I feel with the wrong thought? Now it would make no sense to speak of making the wrong connection unless one could tell from the description given of the tensions which in fact would be the correct connection. Is this description a causal description, *i.e.* is it the description of the impression as the impression that would be dissipated if one got the thing thought about? But in that case one could not say what it is that one wanted unless and until one got it.

112

And, in any case, corresponding to this causal description there must be a further description of the impression. If I say about x rather than z that getting y would remove it, I must surely be able to distinguish x from z. In short, if I am even to say this much about *this* impression rather than *that* one, that getting the caviar would dissipate the former but not the latter, then it must be possible in principle to go on to say what the intrinsic differences between these impressions are.

Assuming then that wanting or desiring is having an impression—some tension, itch, twitch or whatever —how shall we characterize such wantings or desires? How in fact *do* we characterize or describe our desires? Some descriptions are obvious enough but will not do for our present purpose: they can be strong, insistent, fleeting, recurrent, momentary and so on. But if my desire is an internal content or impression, some kind of tension, uneasiness or what-have-you, such descriptions will not enable me to distinguish between the desire for wine and the desire for caviar, since predicates of this sort can be applied equally well to both of them. Here are two embarrassing questions similar to the ones raised in Chapter V concerning the doctrine of acts of volition: How do desires differ in general from other mental events like expecting, hoping, wishing? And how does *this* desire —the one for caviar—differ from *that* one—the desire for wine? It is unnecessary, surely, at this stage to comment at any length upon the resort to indefinables, the move that consists in declaring that desires are indefinably different from other mental events and *this* one indefinably different from *that* one. Enough has been said earlier in Chapter V about this type of obscurantist move. As in the attempt to construe the difference between mere bodily movements and actions in terms of acts of volition, so here in the case of wanting when this is identified with some Humean cause of doing, we are faced with a manifest contradiction. Construed as an internal impression which is thought to function as a cause that issues in some item of so-called overt behaviour (whether this be some bodily movement or an action is of no matter for our present purposes), the impression must be describable without reference to any event or object distinct from it. It must be possible to characterize that internal impression without invoking any reference to the so-called object of the desire, no less than the action that consists either in getting or in trying to get that object. But as a desire, no account is intelligible that does not refer us to the thing desired. The supposition, then, that desiring or wanting is a Humean cause, some sort of internal tension or uneasiness, involves the following contradiction: As Humean cause or internal impression, it must be describable without reference to anything else—object desired, the action of getting or the action of trying to get the thing desired; but as desire this is impossible. Any description of the desire involves a logically necessary connection with the thing desired. No internal impression could possibly have this logical property. Hence, a desire cannot possibly be an internal impression.

This contradiction comes close to the surface in a number of familiar accounts of wanting. Wanting is usually identified with some internal mental event —a felt tension or uneasiness. But as internal event, whether mental or physiological, there is no intrinsic feature of that event that reveals its connection with anything else; yet as desire the very characterization of the desire involves a reference to the thing desired. Hence Hobbes' interesting remark about the intimate relation between names applied to desires and the objects of desire. Shall we then say with G. F. Stout that 'desire and aversion, endeavour to and endeavour from, are modes of attention'?[1] Certainly if there is endeavour to x, there must be attention to x. But if we think of a desire as an internal event that causes or produces an endeavour to the thing in question, then it is self-contradictory to say that the desire is both cause and the attention involved in the endeavour which this cause produces, just as much so as it is for Prichard to say in the case of so-called acts of volition that such acts are causes and also involve the idea of that which they produce. Alternatively, if the desire just *is* the endeavour, it is difficult to see how there could be desire without endeavour, *i.e.* without trying to get the thing desired. But putting this aside, we shall have to say that this endeavour, mental or physiological, involves the idea of that towards which the endeavour is directed—endeavour being necessarily endeavour *to* something, just as a desire is necessarily a desire *for* something. And this implies that the endeavour cannot possibly be a causal factor in the proceedings that issue in the getting of what is desired, since if it were, it would be possible to describe it without referring in any way to anything else in or out of the proceedings, including the thing in question towards which the endeavour is directed.

[1]*Analytic Psychology*, Vol. I, p. 133.

Hobbes and his present-day followers who speak of the endeavours of the body or of physiological drives are similarly involved in contradiction. Physiological occurrences are blind; as such they can be described without reference to anything else including the thing wanted, or the objective of the endeavour. As drives, endeavours or desires, so such logical divorce is possible.

The whole modern picture from Hobbes on down, of wanting or desiring as interior events that operate in some sort of causal mechanism of the mind or body, is in fact a disastrous muddle. So far I have been concerned with this logical feature of a desire, namely, that a desire, whatever else it may be, is a desire *for* something. But there are other important features of the concept of desiring or wanting which this modern picture simply cannot accommodate and which therefore spell disaster for this view of the matter.

It will be remembered that I began this discussion by considering the truism that because one wants or desires one does; in other words, that we explain conduct by reference to, among other things, what agents want or desire. But if desiring is some sort of interior event that functions as a causal condition, no such explanation is possible. Desiring, on this modern view, is some sort of causal factor, an itch, twitch, internal impression, tension or physiological occurrence; but as such, supposing that these are causal factors, it can give rise only to other occurrences. An action, however, is no mere matter of bodily happening. Grant then that wanting or desiring explains the bodily movements that take place when a person does anything, *e.g.* raises his arm in order to signal; as internal

116

occurrence what it explains, at best, is the bodily movement that occurs when the person raises his arm, not the action he performs which we describe as 'raising his arm' or, further, as 'signalling'. A gap then appears in the alleged explanation, between bodily occurrence and action performed, and what is purported to be an explanation of conduct turns out to be nothing of the kind. But like many another gap that appears in philosophy (here readers will be reminded of the familiar gap with which moral philosophers are plagued between the 'is' and the 'ought', between matters of fact and matters of morality, between description and evaluation[1]), this one is a product of our own confusion. Specifically, it is the failure to recognize the *logical* relation between the concept of wanting or desiring and that of action, including the logical scaffolding that gives the latter term its import or use in our language.

Earlier I contended that by no logical alchemy is it possible to make good the claim that an action is a bodily movement plus some other concurrent factor. Suppose, for argument's sake, we take as concurrent factor, wanting or desiring. Then the latter can be understood independently of the concept of the action. If we explain A in terms of B and C, our explanation, if it is to avoid circularity, presupposes that C can be understood without invoking A. So if the action of raising the arm can be understood as the bodily movement incurred in raising the arm together with a desire, one can understand the desire without invoking the idea of this action. This implies that the

[1] Cf. my *Rights and Right Conduct*, Basil Blackwell, Oxford, 1959, p. 72 ff.

desire cannot possibly be the desire to raise one's arm, since it would be circular to define the action of raising one's arm as a bodily movement together with the desire to raise one's arm. But is it possible, in general, to define action as bodily movement or happening plus desire? Only if we can understand what a desire is without invoking the concept of an action. Is this possible? Only if in our account of the action of raising one's arm, we do not invoke any desire to do, *e.g.* the desire to notify others that one is about to make a turn. Or, if we do this, only if we go on to explain a desire to do in terms of a desire together with some feature of the desire which does not involve a reference to doing at all—in which case the desire to do would then be 'reduced' to some sort of occurrence called 'a desire' having a feature that could be described without reference to any doing at all. Now what sort of thing called a 'desire' could this possibly be? Here is one suggestion: the desire is a desire for something, *e.g.* the food that one will get if such-and-such things take place. Let us then see if it is possible to 'explain' the desire *to do* in terms of a desire *for* something. In our example, this then is the situation: One is hungry; food is around the corner, so one notifies others that one is about to make a turn in order to get food; one desires to notify others that one is about to make a turn and one desires to do what is needed in order to get the food; but to say that one desires *to do* these things can be explained or elucidated simply and solely in terms of the presence of a certain occurrence called the desire *for food*. On this suggestion, the notion of desiring to do is elucidated in terms of the logically prior notion of a desire for something.

Here I shall not dwell further upon the now obvious and fatal objection to the identification of the desire for something with some internal occurrence, an objection that is decisive in refuting the contention that an action consists of the dual occurrence of bodily movement and internal event. What I want to examine now is the contention that desires for something are somehow logically more primitive or basic than desires to do, and hence that it is possible to understand the notion of a desire without invoking the concept of an action. There are two questions here: first, is it possible to want or to have a desire for something without wanting to do, and secondly, is it possible that one may have what one wants but not want to do anything with it?

Consider the first question. If I want food but do nothing to get it, that surely is intelligible. I may be unable to get it when, for example, I am tied and gagged. Or, I may do nothing to get it because I am fasting—doctor's orders, you know. Or, I may want this food before me but since it disagrees with me I do nothing to get it. But can I want this food, but not want to do anything to get it? This much is possible: the food is on display in a shop, I have no money, and the only way I can get it is by stealing. Now I do not want to steal—least of all do I want to get it by stealing—let it be that I want to refrain from doing anything that is stealing. Does it follow that I do not want to get the food? Certainly not, since if this did follow it would be logically impossible for anyone to be tempted. The man who is tempted wants to get something despite the fact that by getting it he will be doing the wrong thing; his trouble is that he finds some difficulty in refraining from getting what he wants to get, not that he does not want to get what he wants. If he did not want to get what he wants, it would be impossible for him to be tempted. Nor is it necessary to hold that if a man wants to get food, where getting it would be stealing, that he must be tempted to steal. 'Temptation' is a strong term. The man who is tempted feels the urge to do something to which he has an aversion and must resist it; but a man may want to get something but remain steadfastly in control of his desire and feel no temptation. Now one way of establishing complete self-control is by losing the desire for the thing in question—this in fact is how the man who wants to lose the urge for smoking succeeds. But one may, as in the case of our example of the man who wants food, continue to want it and yet remain free from temptation. If, indeed, we are inclined to deny that if a man wants the food, he must want to get it, this is because of the failure to recognize that, in the particular circumstances, the person would be doing not one thing—getting the food—but at least two things: not only would he be getting the food, but in doing this he would also be stealing. Here we must not say that 'He wants food' logically implies 'He wants to get food' only in certain circumstances (*i.e.* when getting food is not also doing something he wants to avoid doing)—that would be objectionable. We must say rather that in certain circumstances, getting food is also doing what one wants to refrain from doing. Hence, although it follows from the fact that one wants food that one wants to get it, it does not follow that one will want to do what in the given circumstances one will also be doing if one did what one wanted to do. The circumstances determine what it is that one will be doing in getting the food, not the logical connection that holds between wanting the food and wanting to get it. And with respect to what one will be doing in getting what one wants, one's further desires and aversions may, and on occasion do, play a decisive rôle. But given that one does desire food, it is no mere empirical matter dependent upon what else one desires, that one desires to get it. Wanting or desiring anything logically implies wanting or desiring to get it.[1]

Here someone may object in the following way: It is not always possible to get what one wants, nor is it always a small matter. The child wants the moon, but can it want to get it? Certainly, and not in the trivial sense in which 'wanting to get' means wanting to have, but rather in the sense in which this means wanting to do something about obtaining the object wanted, even though nothing it or anyone else can do will be successful in getting it what it wants. And that in wanting the moon it wants to get it—do something about obtaining it—is shown by the fact that it cries for it, or that it says 'I want it'. For here in saying 'I want it', the child is not reporting that it wants, but doing something—summoning help—in the hope that someone else—its parents—will take the necessary steps. Very frequently this is precisely how 'I want . . .' is employed.

But suppose I see a large gold nugget on a narrow ledge high above me on the cliff—surely I may want

[1] I take this to be the import of Kant's remark, in Section II of *The Foundations of the Metaphysics of Morals*, that it is analytic that whoever wills the end wills the indispensably necessary means to it.

it but suffering as I do from vertigo, I do not want to fetch it. And, if so, it would seem that wanting the nugget cannot logically imply wanting to get it; unless 'wanting to get' means wanting to have, in which case the alleged logical implication reduces to barren triviality: wanting the object logically implies wanting to have it, *i.e.* wanting it. But wanting to get is wanting to do something in order to obtain possession, not necessarily wanting to fetch it; and one way of doing something is to hire someone else to fetch it for me. But suppose that this is impossible; I have no idea how to obtain the nugget except by fetching it myself —something I most certainly do not want to do. Unlike the child who thinks that its parents can reach and give it the moon it wants, I see no way of being able to get it. But I still want the nugget. And seeing that it is beyond my power to get it, do I still want to get it?

Now a person may be powerless to do anything that would give him possession of what he wants, but still want it—indeed he may even try to get it if mistakenly he thinks he can do something to obtain it. But must he, if he wants the thing, *believe* that he can get it? That is much too strong. Suppose I try to dislodge the nugget by hitting it with a rock—I need not believe that I shall hit it but only hope that by chance I shall hit it and knock it off the ledge. But suppose, further, I even cease to try to hit it—it seems hopeless to try to get it that way—do I thereby cease to want the nugget and even to want to do something that will enable me to get my hands on it? Consider the case of a bowler who has just released the ball but who sees it veering off from the pin at which he aimed it—

surely he may still want to have it hit the pin even though really he does not either believe or hope that this will occur. And just as in this case, so in the case in which I see the tantalizing nugget above me, I still want the thing and want to do whatever is needed to get it. For just as the bowler shows that he wants by his demeanour—he twists his body as if thereby to change the path taken by the ball; so in my thoughts and in my behaviour I show that I want the nugget —I consider wildly impossible ways of getting it, stare at it in fascination, etc., etc. It may be that the bowler's contortions are the last vestiges of some long-forgotten superstitious belief that one can, barely by thinking of what one wants, alter the course of natural events, and that I, in remaining on the scene and thinking about wildly absurd methods of getting the nugget, am unreasonable. Nevertheless, in these cases there is wanting. And the fact that in these examples there is wanting rather than idle wishing for the object in question is shown in the bowler's absurd contortions and in my wild conjectures and in my behaviour. Wanting would degenerate into idle wishing if not only all hope of getting were abandoned but also all effort and all thought of how the thing wanted could be obtained. We should have idle wish if in either example the agent merely reflected upon the agreeable features of having what was wanted, and only if the agent no longer showed by his thought and his action that he wanted to do something to get what he wanted.

It is then quite impossible to suppose that the concept of wanting can be understood in logical independence of the concept of doing. But we must now examine the second of the two questions I raised, that pertaining to the relation between having what one has wanted—one has now gotten it—and doing.

This much is possible: A child may say, 'I want this' but when given it, do nothing with it—if it is an apple, it may look at it for a moment, and then pay no further attention to it. Must it have been untruthful? Certainly not. It may have wanted it, but its attention may have been diverted to something else and so it may no longer want it. Or, what it really wanted, was not the apple but attention—this is familiar enough to parents. Or, it may have wanted an apple, but *this* one will not do—it is yellow, not red; dull, not shiny; or in some other way not a good one at all. Or, it may want this one, but drop it—it wants the apple but does not want to submit to the humiliating way in which it was given it. Just so a hungry man may do nothing with the food he is given, if in being given the food he is treated like a beggar and in accepting it he demeans himself, or if he is too proud to acknowledge the void in both his stomach and purse, and so on. But suppose that there is nothing of this sort: he wants the food, gets it, no other want, interest of his prevents him from eating it, yet he does nothing with it. Even this is intelligible. The food being a sculptured cake or ice, he may want simply to look at it in admiration; and a miser may want as much soap as possible but never use it in the familiar way and only rub his hands in glee as he gapes at his growing hoard. But certainly it would make no sense to suppose that someone has what he wants but does not want it *for anything* at all, whether to look at it with glee or interest or pleasure or to do something else with it. If

124

it is food that he wants, he surely wants to do something when he has it. It would be self-contradictory to say that he wanted food but did not want it for anything at all, not even to look at. That in point of fact he did not look at it or use it in the familiar way would show decisively, granted that he wanted the food, not that he did not want it for anything at all, but that looking at it or using it would in the particular circumstances *also* be doing something else he wished to avoid doing. Looking at it might be showing too much interest in the food, eating it might be showing callousness to the hunger of others staring at the food, and so on. In short, just as wanting something entails wanting to get it, so having what one wants logically implies wanting to do something with it. This indeed is the only point to one criticism of Butler on hunger, namely, that *really* one does not want food, but the eating of it. Of course the hungry man, no less than the war-time hoarder of food, wants food—so far Butler is perfectly correct—but unlike the latter he wants it for the eating, a fact one should hope that Butler would never have wished to deny.

I have been calling attention to the logical involvement of desiring with doing. In this respect desiring or wanting is unlike wishing—there can be an idle wish but what would an idle desire be? One the object of which it would be foolish to get because it would do no good? But that would be a foolish desire. An idle wish is one in which there is no desire to get the thing wished for; *e.g.* the man who sits back and neither does anything about it nor has any inclination to do so and who says, 'How I wish I were a millionaire', is expressing an idle wish. Of course a man may

125

feel the itch of desire and yet not do anything. But this does not show that desiring is some internal going-on, intelligible independently of any reference to doing. The term 'itch' is useful here precisely because an itch is something about which it is difficult to resist doing something, namely, scratching. So too with terms like 'urge' and 'crave'. Far from supporting the view that desiring is some internal impression the whole point of such figures of speech is to emphasize the connection of the concept of desire with that of action, by marking the restraint necessary to refrain from getting or trying to get what is wanted.

CHAPTER ELEVEN

WANTING TO DO AND DOING

IN the preceding chapter I argued that wanting a thing logically implies wanting to get it, and, since wanting a thing is always wanting it for something, that having what one wants logically implies wanting to do something with it. Quite apart from the fact that one does not always do what one wants to do, it should be clear that any attempt to define 'action' in terms of wanting is hopelessly circular: 'wanting' or 'desiring' like 'motive' is intelligible only against a background understanding of 'doing'. But this is not enough. We need to ask now why it is, given that one has the thing one wants, one not only wants to do but often at least does something with it.

The familiar answer is that the wanting or desiring is an internal event that produces the doing. Aristotle, for example, speaks of the desire as an efficient cause that moves one's bodily parts. Similarly, modern philosophers from Hobbes on down to the present day, treat desire as some sort of psychological or physiological event that sparks bodily movements into being. On this view the relation between desire and the so-called overt behaviour is causal; and conceivably, therefore, one could want but never do since, after all, that one does *because* one desires, is a causal and hence contingent matter.

A moment's reflection will suffice to show that this is patent nonsense. If the relation were causal, the wanting to do would be, indeed it must be, describable independently of any reference to the doing. But it is logically essential to the wanting that it is the wanting to do something of the required sort with the thing one has. Hence the relation between the wanting to do and the doing cannot be a causal one.

Further, the whole idea of the wanting as an internal event that plays a causal rôle in the operations of the mind or body simply will not square with our notion that wanting or desiring, like doing, is subject to rational appraisal. As an internal happening in the mechanism of the mind or body, its connection with anything worthwhile becomes wholly fortuitous. For, so far, there is none of the logical setting for the appraisal of the desire as reasonable or unreasonable, since as internal happening the desire occurs in and to one for causes of its own; and if it produces anything desirable, that does not establish the desire as reasonable but only as fortunate in its consequences.

Besides, what can the wanting, so conceived, produce? A happening can only produce other happenings. Hence even if, when a man wants food and sees that it can be obtained in the restaurant across the street, the wanting may excite the movement of legs, but will it explain his doing, namely, his action of walking across the street to get it? It is futile to attempt to explain conduct through the causal efficacy of desire—all *that* can explain is further happenings, not actions performed by agents. The agent confronting

128

the causal nexus in which such happenings occur is a helpless victim of all that occurs in and to him. There is no place in this picture of the proceedings either for rational appraisal or desires, or even for the conduct that was to have been explained by reference to them.

It may be objected that the man who wants does have thoughts concerning the desirability of the thing, that he is not helpless in the face of the desires that move him, since the thoughts he has are determining factors in what happens. It is not then a future good that moves him to act but a present thought of a future good. This thought is subject to rational appraisal as either true or false; and the reasonable man is one who checks his desires or releases them by means of the thoughts he has concerning the good to be obtained or the evil to be avoided. But granted that my thoughts, and I for having them, are subject to rational appraisal, how do these move? As Aristotle himself remarked, 'Intellect itself . . . moves nothing' (*Nicomachean Ethics*, 1139a). How can reason thus conceived be practical? Self-styled Humeans who adopt such bland measures in order to explain purposive action in causal terms seem to be oblivious to this ancient conundrum; Hume himself saw the force of the objection and adopted the heroic measure of attempting to show how, in accordance with the principles of human nature, a thought could, in special circumstances, become a passion and thus function as a causal factor. But for those loath to adopt Hume's extreme measures the appeal to the consideration that thought operates as a causal factor in the proceedings, in which a man wants and either does or refrains from doing, creates a nightmare of confusions. How can intellect move a man to do or, given that he wants to do something with the thing he has, check the steeds of desire? And even if it could do this, even if we pile one incredible supposition upon another and suppose that a thought is some sort of event in a causal chain, how does this forestall the conclusion that one is a helpless victim of all that happens in and to one, the thoughts no less than the desires and other factors that either issue in or fail to issue in conduct? Indeed, what conduct can such occurrences produce? All that they can do is to produce further happenings, perhaps the movement of muscles and limbs, but these surely are not actions. In short, the 'explanation' succeeds only in changing the subject. But suppose that a man is not helpless in the thoughts he has—these are not inextricably bound up in a causal nexus in which they occur as effects of antecedent events—then *he* thinks as he does. This, then, is presumably something he does. His thoughts, then, are no mere events that happen in and to him, and which come and go through the operation of the laws of causality or association. But as such they are no longer causal factors, happenings, but *doings*. And as doings they are remarkable instances of our butting into the complex causal nexus of events that happen in and to us. How do *I*, by thinking, affect the natural history of the events that happen in and to me? And even if I succeeded in doing that much, how do I, by thinking, affect my conduct, my actions? It is a remarkable example of philosophical myopia that these difficulties in the old idea of a desire as that which produces movement have been so very largely ignored.

It is implausible in the extreme to argue that the source of these difficulties is the verbal consideration that we do speak of a man being moved by desire. Our philosophical tendencies may be prompted by such idioms, but they cannot be sustained by them. Nor is it merely that our conception of the rôle of desire in conduct is a product of our obsession with the causal picture of natural occurrences—ironically enough this picture is a considerable modern achievement in freeing the account of natural phenomena from just such concepts of purpose and desire that are in fact applicable to human conduct. No doubt modern philosophers have been moved by the hope that the concepts and methods successfully employed in the physical sciences could be extended to the sphere of thought and action. But why should this hope be attractive, even compulsive? The answer to this question is intimately connected with a tempting move we examined earlier and rejected: How can one tell that one is raising one's arm when one is not observing oneself doing so?[1] Here the demand for evidence, data on the basis of which one is able to say without looking, 'Now I am raising my arm', stems from the idea that thought is essentially contemplative, that if one has knowledge one's thoughts must agree with something independent of the thoughts. And here again, the gap between one's arm rising and one's raising one's arm threatens to raise havoc with this requirement of knowledge. For granted that one does have evidence, how can that evidence assure one that one is raising one's arm, not merely that one's arm is rising? Must we not say that here the knowledge one

[1] Cf. Chapter V.

131

has is involved in the doing one performs—by making the proposition true that one is raising one's arm, *i.e.* by doing, one knows that one is raising one's arm. Similarly, if it is asked, 'How can reason be practical?', the idea behind the question is that it is the office of reason to contemplate or discover matters of fact or the relations of ideas—in the case of conduct, to contemplate events that pass before its view. Whatever happens happens not because of what reason contributes to the scene—all it can do is to pick out events, recognize correlations, make predictions and offer explanations —and let it recognize if it can that the outcome of these events will be fortunate or unfortunate, that recognition will make no difference to what takes place. For what happens happens not because it is known to happen but because of antecedent causal factors. One might just as well suppose that a spectator at a rodeo, observing a rider on a bucking bronco, could make a difference to the outcome by means of the reliable predictions he is able to make. But not only is reason thus helpless in the face of the events that pass before its view, including the desires that come and go in their causal relations, even actions themselves (as distinct from mere happenings) disappear from view. How can reason, as an observer of the passing scene, discover anything except happenings? Hence arise the desperate attempts we have examined and rejected to distinguish between actions and mere happenings in terms of the order of causes—acts of volitions, motives and even desires, these being construed as causal factors. How indeed can reason be practical if reason as a mere observer of happenings cannot so much as discover any actions at all? The idea that

132

desires are internal occurrences that produce movements stems from this sterile conception of reason.

Here we need to recover our sense that a human being is an agent no less than a spectator; that rationality is as much a feature of wanting and doing as it is of thinking; indeed, that rationality begins with the practical knowledge involved in doing. The familiar view is that intelligence begins with the recognition of colours, shapes and other qualities given in sensation; that given such abstracted qualities we come to identify objects as arms, legs, hands, rattles, cribs, etc.; that given such identifications, correlations are then made between the movements of these objects; that discoveries are then made about the ways in which certain movements, *e.g.* the movements of arms, hands, rattles, etc., may be brought to pass; and that in this way the infant learns how to do things with the objects before it. We have explored the incoherences involved in the idea that one learns to move one's limbs by performing internal actions that produce bodily movements. But even if *per impossibile* this could take place, it would be preposterous to ascribe such intellectual discoveries to the young infant. Nor is it even true that we first learn to pick out qualities and then identify the objects about us by means of them. The history of philosophy is surely instructive here—the trail of fatal difficulties in the various attempts to make good this conception of our knowledge of objects should warn us that something is amiss in this account. Fortunately it is unnecessary for our purposes to engage in an excursion into epistemology, into a discussion of the fatal logical blunder involved in the philosophical idea of a pure intelligence.

Our concern is with the fact that we do have practical knowledge, that human beings are agents and that they and their desires may be appraised as reasonable or unreasonable. If these matters are to be understood our starting point is not the contemplation of events and the discovery of methods by which an intelligence may secure effects—this, as I have argued, is a hopeless beginning—but rather the practical contexts in which actions are performed and in which an agent does things with the objects about him. We do not ask, 'How can reason be practical?', *i.e.* 'How can action get started?' Only where there is action can there be intelligence and wanting. How indeed could reason fail to be practical in the practical situations in which an agent does things with the objects about him?

Consider the simple case in which one moves one's arm. One can do this, of course, without attending to what one is doing and for no reason whatsoever. Indeed, 'moving one's arm' is a description that fits an immensely varied set of cases. And where shall we draw the line between cases to which we apply this description of an action and those to which the expression 'bodily movement' is more apt? Here we have ever so many different sorts of borderline cases: a human being half asleep or coming out of narcosis, an infant who is not wholly devoid of the primitive ability to move its limbs at will, a madman—in these and many other cases the distinction between action and bodily movement is blurred; and where we can speak of wanting as playing a rôle in the doing that occurs, some of the features of the concept of wanting which are exhibited in the rational attentive behaviour of human beings are surely missing. Here we need not a formula—which not only ignores the fine shadings and the borderline cases that exist, but in being designed to fit the great variety of cases we encounter suffers from intolerable vagueness—but rather attention to clear-cut standard cases of an agent who is intelligent in and attentive to what he is doing. For it is by reference to such cases that we come to grasp the important logical relations of wanting and doing. In the case of an infant who does not have control of its limbs, we have neither attention nor inattention, neither acting for a reason nor acting without a reason, neither wanting or doing itself. Let us then consider a standard case of an agent who can indeed raise his arm, mindful of what he is doing and for a reason—here the concepts of wanting and doing are applicable in a wholly untruncated manner, in all of their rich logical texture.

Now the supposition that such an agent *always* acts inattentively and for no reason at all is not false but self-contradictory. Of such an agent it may be false to say that he is *always* attentive to what he is doing and that he *always* acts as he does for a reason, but it is not self-contradictory. But we could not describe such a being as acting for no reason at all and without attending to what he is doing unless, in many cases at least, he did in fact act attentively and for a reason. Here someone might object that certain animals (*e.g.* a crab hunting instinctively for food) act as they do without thinking, without plan or purpose; that all that we need for the intelligibility of 'acting inattentively and for no reason' is the intelligibility of the contrasting expression 'acting attentively and for a reason'—not actual cases to which the latter applies; and, finally, that it would be absurd to suppose that it is logically necessary that there be attentive intelligent agents or the actions of such agents that are describable in these same terms. Now I am not arguing the logically trivial point that an attentive and intelligent agent acts attentively and intelligently, that it is self-contradictory to assert that such an agent never acts attentively and rationally. And I shall not press the verbal point that we do not in fact apply the description 'acting thoughtlessly and for no reason' to beings devoid of intelligence or rationality—a crab, for example, is unthinking, not thoughtless. Nor should I want to assert that it is logically necessary that there be higher forms of animal life or human beings who are rational in and attentive to what they are doing. It is rather that we must start from the fact that we do have the concepts of agent, wanting and doing; that these are exhibited in their full logical structure in the lives and actions of intelligent attentive beings; that we have these full-bodied concepts precisely because they apply to the incidents of our own lives in which we act as we do, in very many cases at least, fully mindful of what we are doing and for reasons that we can cite and understand. These are not theoretical concepts whose applicability to events can be a matter of speculation—they are, rather, practical concepts which we are able to grasp precisely because we ourselves are agents of the kind in question who can and often do act with full attention to what we are doing and for good reason. Starting, then, as we do, with *our* concepts—for it is with these that we are concerned and not the trun-

cated ones we apply, for example, to the crab scurry-
ing for food—it is self-contradictory to suppose that
in our full-bodied sense of these terms there could be
agents who never act attentively and for a reason.
Only a person who has mastered a language and who
has communicated, *i.e.* has told the truth, can lie;
similarly only a person who has been attentive can
be said to act for no reason and without attending to
what he is doing.[1] In the former case what is given as
the starting point is a language one has learned to
use, with respect to which the improprieties are intelligible only as deviations from the standard; in the
latter case what we must start with is an agent who
is intelligent in, and attentive to, what he is doing
with the things that interest him—acting inattentively
or for no reason at all are intelligible only as deviants
from this.

Still, such an agent as we have been considering
might raise his arm but not want to do so, and he
might want to raise his arm but refrain from doing so.
But is it possible that he might never do what he
wants to do or that he might always do what he does
not want to do? In order to answer these questions
we need to look more closely at 'attending to what one
does' and 'doing for a reason'.

Consider a full-blown case in which one raises one's
arm where both of these descriptions apply. To what
must one attend when one raises one's arm? Surely
not just to the action of raising one's arm. Suppose I
am being examined by a physician and he tells me to
raise my arm—he is examining my chest or shoulders;

[1] Hence the correctness of Kant's insistence that universalized
lying is self-contradictory.

and promptly I proceed to smash his spectacles as I bring my arm up over my head. Is *this* being attentive to what I am doing? Attending to what I am doing is being mindful of the circumstances in which I perform the action of raising my arm. If I attend to what I am doing when, as I drive my car, I move my limbs to steer, shift or brake the car, surely it is not these bodily actions to which I attend, but to the relevant circumstances in which these actions are performed—these may be, for example, the tricky gearbox or the conditions on the road. Normally, we do not attend to the bodily actions we perform when we attend to what we are doing, but to the circumstances in which the bodily action is performed; to the physician who asks me to raise my arm, to the condition of the car or the traffic on the road, or, in the case of an infant reaching for a rattle, to the rattle above it as it raises its arm. The reason for this is that in these circumstances, to which the agent attends, the action of raising one's arm is also an action of a different sort. The action I perform is not only that of raising my arm, but co-operating with the examining physician. The action of a child is both that of raising its arm and reaching for a bauble. The action of grasping the lever and pushing it forward is the action of shifting gears, and so on. Since the action of raising one's arm, in the given circumstances, is also an action of another sort —co-operating with the physician, shifting gears, reaching for a bauble—attending to what one is doing, by attending to the circumstances in which one is raising one's arm, is knowing what one is doing *in* raising one's arm. But this knowing is not a matter of observing what one is doing in raising one's arm—if

138

it were, observing what one is doing would logically imply observing the bodily action of raising one's arm. For the very same event which is the action of raising one's arm is also, in the circumstances to which one is attending, the action of, say, co-operating with the physician, shifting gears or reaching for a bauble. Nor is this knowing what one is doing a case of discovering what one is doing in the way in which a man might discover that absent-mindedly he has been trying to put the left shoe on his right foot. Still less is this knowledge inferential: I am raising my arm, raising my arm in these circumstances is, say, obliging the physician, *ergo*, I am obliging the physician. One can say that the person knows by doing, that he knows that he is doing what he is doing by making that proposition true. In saying this one must not suppose that one is answering the question 'How does he know?', *i.e.* 'Upon what data, evidence or information is his knowledge based?' Rather, one must understand by this that here there is a rock-bottom matter involved in the very concept of an agent—one who by using his limbs is able to do things in the presence of and with the things to which he attends. This is not a matter to be explained in terms of something else—rather it is our starting point in any explanation we give of conduct.

But can a person attend to circumstances in which he acts without recognizing some matters of fact? And if he must discover some truths in order to have this so-called practical knowledge of the action he is performing in raising his arm, is it not true that in order to do anything with the objects before him a person must have sensation and, with it, the much-abused contemplative knowledge of fact? Here we need to remember that the logical starting point in our account is the case of a person who is not only attentive to what he is doing, but also doing what he is doing for a reason. But if he has a reason for raising his arm, there must be something he wants which he can get by doing this—in the case of the man who raises his arm for the examining physician, health. And that to which he attends, namely, the request of the physician, he attends because of his concern with his health. It is of course true that even on a common-sense level we can and do take notice of events that do not concern or even interest us; we can be passive spectators whose desires and interests are in no way bound up with the things we observe. These, however, are sophisticated performances that are possible only because we have acquired the ability to attend to the things we want and to the things that interest and concern us—the objects and events that please or distress us, that excite our curiosity or our fancy and to which we respond by reaching, touching and grasping. Intelligence begins with attention to things that arouse our interest and concerns, with respect to which we are not passive spectators but responsive agents. Sensation, attention and observation on the primitive level of an infant's experience are inseparable from volition and action. Only when these functions of intelligence have been achieved can there be that function of intelligence in which there is no desire, not even the desire to satisfy one's curiosity. But if one is attending to what one is doing in raising one's arm, certainly one is attending to things that interest one, and if one is raising one's arm for a reason, then there is something wanted which one supposes one would gain or might gain by raising one's arm—clearly one would have no reason for raising one's arm unless in doing so one thought one might get the thing one wanted, *e.g.* health, attention, relaxation of one's muscles or whatever. It follows that it is logically impossible that one should want but never do, or that one should never do what one wants to do. For where there is wanting there is an agent who does; where there is doing there is an agent who can be and has been attentive to what he is doing and who acts as he does for a reason; where there is doing for a reason there it is false that one does what one does not want to do. If it is self-contradictory to suppose that a person could always act without attention to what he does and for no reason whatsoever, it is self-contradictory to suppose that he never does what he wants to do, namely, to get the thing he wants and, when he gets it, to do the thing he wants to do with it.

Yet on a given occasion a man may want something yet do nothing to get it, or if he is given it do nothing with it. On the familiar view, this is put down to the fact that there are causal conditions which interfere with the normal causal efficacy of desire. The true account of the matter, however, must be given in terms of the intelligence exhibited by the agent in his abstentions.

In the previous chapter I argued that the fact that a person wants something entails that he wants to get it and the fact that an agent has what he wants entails that he wants to do something with it, despite the fact that he may do nothing in the former case to get it or in the latter case with the thing he wants and has. The explanation I offered is that in the former case the action of getting the thing wanted, in the latter case the action of doing something with the thing, *e.g.* eating it if it is food, may also be, in the particular circumstances then present, an action the agent wants to refrain from doing. Getting the thing wanted may be, for example shirking one's duty; eating the food one wants and has may be attracting unwanted attention or depriving others of food they need desperately. Failure to recognize the fact that an action Y performed by executing a bodily movement X may in specific circumstances be an action Z, vitiates a good deal of controversy by moral philosophers who argue the pros and cons of the contention that what makes an action right are its desirable consequences. For of course everything depends upon *what* the action is. An act by which one takes the life of another human being may be, depending upon particular circumstances, carrying out one's soldierly duties or self-defence or murder; and failure to recognize this fact has given rise to the morally offensive suggestion and surely very confused idea that any action, even murder, may be justified only by appealing to consequences.[1] But to return to the main point—a man may not do what he wants to do and for a very good reason, this being a matter that has to do, not with any facts of causality, but rather with what he is concerned and hence with what he thinks to be desirable or undesirable to do in the particular circumstances in which he is placed. The circumstances may indeed be enormously complicated. They may and often do involve the actions, abstentions, expec-

[1] Cf. my *Rights and Right Conduct*, Section XI.

tations and interests of others no less than of his own, matters of proprieties—moral, legal and otherwise— with which he is concerned and which affect the desirability of getting what he wants and of using the thing he wants once he has it. But these circumstances will determine whether or not he acts precisely because they determine what the character of the action under these circumstances is, and, given the agent's concerns with and attitudes towards actions of that character, may determine whether or not he wants to act in that sort of way. He wants food for the pleasure of eating, but getting it in particular circumstances may be depriving others of food they need far more desperately than he does; and although he may want to get it, he may refrain from doing so precisely because he wants far more to help others—this being a desirable end—than to eat the food for the pleasure it gives him.

It hardly needs to be emphasized that wanting or desiring are not restricted in their application to bodily appetites, still less are they to be identified with bodily depletions or tensions, *i.e.* the so-called bodily needs. For even when a man wants food when he is hungry, his wanting food is one thing and his bodily needs—what is required by his body for its continued efficiency—is something else again; a man may be hungry but not want food. And it is conceivable that he may be hungry but not require food for the continued efficiency of the body or for whatever else may be required by the bodily mechanism when a man is hungry. The things wanted by a person are a reflection of his interests and of the sort of agent he is—they extend far beyond the range of his bodily appetites and needs.

CHAPTER TWELVE

WANTING TO DO,
REASONS FOR DOING, DOING

IN the preceding chapter I explored some of the logical relations between wanting and doing. I argued that 'wanting' or 'desiring' can be understood only by learning how to apply these terms to intelligent and attentive agents in the transactions in which they engage with the things about them. They do not mark interior events that are natural causes of bodily movements or actions—hence the logical incoherence, and no mere violation of empirical fact, involved in the supposition that a person might never do what he wants to do or always do what he does not want to do. But if we are to take account of some of the more important features of the concept of wanting or desiring, we need to look more closely at the logical connections between desiring and the desirable, reasons for doing, and also at the respects in which a person's desires may explain and may be exhibited in his conduct.

According to one familiar doctrine, the difference between the desired and the desirable is the difference between a matter of psychological fact and something logically independent of it, namely, a matter of value.

Borrowing from Hume, some writers would declare that we cannot move from the 'is desired' to the 'is desirable', since the latter introduces a new mode of predication or a new relation of ideas; and some would hold that in order to pass from 'X is desired' to 'X is desirable', the very questionable major premise, 'Whatever is desired is desirable' would be required. It seems to follow from this account that one can fully understand the notion of desiring without in any way invoking the notion of desirability, that there is no logical absurdity involved in the supposition that a man may want anything at all. To put it in Humean terms, it is not contrary to reason that a man should want the extinction of his or anyone's life, of the universe itself. That in general we do not want such undesirables is a fortunate and contingent matter. Conceivably—and this would involve nothing logically impossible—all men might always want the ridiculous and even the undesirable.

I want to argue that this is a mistake. One can on occasion desire the undesirable—there is nothing self-contradictory in that—but from this it does not follow that there is no logical connection between the desired and the desirable. Consider parallel cases: Some works of art do not have merit. It does not follow from the fact that something is a work of art that it has merit. But it would be ridiculous to argue on this account that there is no logical connection between the concept of a work of art and the concept of merit. A work of art is precisely the sort of thing created with the view of achieving the merit appropriate to it—we should not understand something being called a work of art with respect to which the question of merit is ruled out,

145

as indeed it is in the case of the rocks on the hillside
or the clouds in the sky. These can be striking, even
beautiful, but they do not have merit. Or to take another example: it is possible to punish an innocent
man. But it would be a logical howler to infer from
this all-too-familiar fact that there is no logical connection between the concepts of punishment and guilt.
The supposition that the innocent are never punished
is intelligible, but is it equally intelligible that the
innocent and only the innocent have been and always
will be punished? Similarly, it is intelligible that only
desirable things are desired, but is it equally intelligible that men never desire what is desirable since
anything whatever, without restriction, conceivably
might be desired?

Let us return once more to what we took as our
starting point, an agent mindful of what he is doing
and acting as he does for a reason. Suppose such an
agent driving along the street and suddenly coming
to a stop at the curb. His companion asks, 'Why are
you stopping here?' The answer, 'There is a restaurant
nearby', may be true, but the statement, while it may
inform his companion of a matter of fact, is not offered
as a mere statement of fact in the way in which, for
example, this might be done if the persons had been
concerned to compile a report of the distribution of
restaurants in that locality. It is offered rather as a
reason for *doing* something, namely, stopping the car.
But 'There is a restaurant nearby' would be no reason
for stopping the car unless there was something wanted
and to be gotten by performing that action—one stops
the car in order to go into the restaurant, and one does
that in order to get food. And if one wants food, pre-

146

sumably (although not necessarily) one wants it for the eating. Normally, the reason given, 'There is a restaurant nearby', will make it clear that one is stopping the car in order to get the food one wants to eat. And in many cases at least, stating a reason for what one is doing is making it clear what it is that is wanted and what it is that one wants to do with the thing wanted. That it does this depends of course on our common understanding of people, and on our knowledge of their circumstances—in our example, on the knowledge that it is time for lunch, that the driver is normal in his eating habits and interests (he eats at the regular times and is not dieting or fasting, etc., etc.). But equally and with the same effect, the driver might have replied, 'I am hungry', or, 'It is time for lunch', or simply, 'I want to eat', which would have explained the action of stopping the car as a case of stopping the car at the restaurant in order to obtain the food wanted. In all of these cases, the reason given explains the action of stopping the car by exhibiting it, in the given circumstances, as a case of getting what was wanted. The choice of the specific answer given will be governed, generally, by the manner in which one chooses to fill in the details of the circumstances surrounding the action.

If one wants a thing, must one believe that the thing wanted is desirable? Or, to put it in Aristotelian terms, is good the object of desire just as truth is the object of opinion? Surely not. Normally one wants food not because one thinks it good for one but because one is hungry; but to say that one wants food because one is hungry is not to justify but to explain oneself—one is making it clear that one's response to food is that of a hungry person. 'Why do you want . . .?' may be answered by explaining that one wants to indulge one's passing fancy or whim, but such a reply never serves to justify one's desire as reasonable, and with it the action of getting the thing wanted. To say 'I just feel like it' in reply to such a question as 'Why do you want to watch the T.V.?' is precisely to make it clear that there is no justification involved; yet it does explain why it is that one does want to watch the T.V.—one just feels like doing so, Period.[1] It would be excessively intellectualistic to suppose that every case of an intelligent want or desire must be a case of a want or desire for some envisaged good. If, for example, I have reason for changing my clothes, namely, to prepare to go out into the garden, it by no means follows that if I am pressed by the question 'Why?', I must terminate my replies by some reference to a good to be achieved. For, why go out into the garden? Here the answer might well be 'To potter'. And why that? Surely 'I just feel like it' ends the matter. Here I have a reason which does not justify but surely does explain my changing my clothes.

A reason for doing, then, may or may not be a justification. In many of the incidents of our lives, one's reason for doing something (*e.g.* stopping at the restaurant, changing one's clothes, etc.) is that this will enable one to do something one wants to do (get the food one wants to eat, potter in the garden, etc.). And the fact that 'I just feel like it' (so too with 'This is the "done" thing' and other 'stoppers') brings us to the end of the line in the explanations of one's conduct

[1] I owe the recognition of the importance of this example to Professor A. E. Murphy.

by no means implies that in these everyday incidents one is irrational or unintelligent. Similarly it does not establish that one is unmindful of what one is doing or inattentive to the circumstances in which one is performing one's actions. An intelligent, rational being need not be justified in everything he does, nor need he, failing such justification, lapse into eccentricity, madness, inattention or stupidity. On the contrary, there would be something forbidding about a human being who *always* felt it necessary to be justified in everything he did, or who was concerned with some good to be achieved in or by all of his doings. But to say that in these familiar incidents one has come to the end of the line must not be misunderstood. If someone explains his action by reference to what he wants and in reply to the question 'Why do you want to do *that*?' simply says 'I just feel like it', it by no means follows that all further inquiry of any sort is ruled out. Why, for example, do persons just feel like pottering in gardens, looking at the T.V. or dancing? Here one can, no doubt, offer various explanations of the manner in which persons develop and exhibit their whims, passing fancies, likes, skills, etc.

However, it is not every conceivable doing with respect to which 'I just feel like it' provides us with the requisite understanding of a person and his conduct. Suppose, for example, someone is collecting faggots on a very hot day and busily engaged in carrying them into his house. Why is he doing that? Well, he might be doing it in order to prepare for the winter —faggots are useful in starting fires and so he is getting ready for the winter in this way. But suppose his answer is that he is piling them into his bedroom from floor to ceiling, and from wall to wall. This too is intelligible but here we are likely to be hard pressed to understand him. Is he doing this as a joke, to prepare the way for a novel but effective way of burning down his house and collecting the insurance, and so on with other unusual but possibly applicable explanations? But suppose that in reply to 'Why?' he rejects all of these explanations and says seriously, 'No reason at all—I just feel like it.' Is this intelligible? 'No reason at all—I just feel like it' is an intelligible form of words. But it is intelligible only insofar as it can be employed by agents in explaining themselves and their doings. Such explanations of persons and their doings do not occur *in vacuo*; they depend upon a background understanding we have of them as normal, intelligent and rational beings with whom we can carry on our everyday social dealings. But here we can only gape—there is no such background understanding that enables us to understand what is going on—we simply would not understand a person who under these circumstances said 'No reason at all—I just feel like it'. And we should write him off as mad or as a strange unintelligible being since he has rejected any possible explanation that might have occurred to us and has insisted upon a 'No reason at all—I just feel like it' that leaves us as completely in the dark about himself and his conduct as we were when we began to question him.

Earlier I argued that we must take as the starting point in our account of action and volition the case of an agent who is attentive and rational. The reason for this is that our concepts of acting and wanting are practical concepts which apply to beings like ourselves who not only dawdle, amuse themselves, act as they do not only because they feel like it, but also for all sorts of reasons including those that fully justify them in their conduct. Actions, and the desires that explain them, are of course the actions and desires *of agents*; but this prepositional phrase does far more than indicate an identifiable subject or owner. Rather, it serves to mark the logically important point that the character of the concepts of action and desire and the kind of agent—man or animal—are reciprocally dependent upon one another. It is for this reason that the consideration 'What shall we make of a man who stuffs his room with faggots, for no reason at all?' is crucially important. The fact that were this to occur we should be utterly bewildered shows that important features of our familiar concepts of both action and agent simply will not fit this case—we would not understand the action because we simply could not understand such an agent.

If, then, we are to take due account of the circumstances to which the concepts of action and desire are employed, the supposition that a person might *never* desire something for the good in it—that no matter what it is that he wanted to do with anything he desired, his answer to the question 'Why do you want . . .?' would be 'No reason at all, I just felt like it'— this supposition, I say, is incoherent. For here, every question 'What's the good in the thing you want?', would be ruled out as inapplicable. Such a being, in all of its so-called doings, would be indifferent to any good or evil, whether natural, social, moral or intellectual. No reason for any of its 'doings' that would seem to justify them could be given by or for it. Pain punishment, death itself, could not deter it; it would have no reason to do or to abstain from doing in order to avoid these evils, since if it did, then it would want to do, or to abstain from doing, because of the evils thereby to be avoided. Not even of an animal to which, albeit in a truncated way, we apply the concepts of action and desire could this be true. In short, we should be totally baffled by the 'doings' of a being of this sort; for here there is no adequate logical foothold for the application of our concepts of agent, action and desire. The supposition that a human being—one we can understand and hence one to whose doings our action concepts are applicable—never desires to do because of the desirability of so doing is logically impossible. The linguistic connection of 'desired' and 'desirability' is, then, no accident—it stems from an important connection of ideas.

Let us turn next to a more detailed consideration of the explanation of conduct in terms of the desires of the agent. Here it is important that we recognize the rôle of intention and the manner in which an agent's desires may be explained by his intentions. Consider the case of an intentional action one does not want to do, *e.g.* raising one's arm in order to signal a turn when one is kidnapped and forced to obey the instruction to do so. Raising one's arm is intentional but not something one wants to do. Yet in these circumstances, doing this is also something else— preserving one's life, something one considers worth- while—which justifies the intentional action of raising the arm. Earlier I maintained that if a person wants something, he wants to do whatever he considers necessary in order to get it. Here, however, he wants to preserve his life, but he is forced to, he does not want to, do what is required in order to get what above all else he wants, namely, the preservation of his life. Is there a contradiction here? Must we now say that our kidnapped man must really want to drive and to raise his arm in order to give the signal?

Surely not. Raising his arm *is* giving the signal. Our man does not want to raise his arm and thus give the signal. Neither does he want to drive. But doing these things in the given circumstances is preserving his life —something he wants and considers worthwhile. Here it is all-important that we recognize that an action X, in given circumstances, may also be an action Y of a quite different sort. Everything depends, therefore, on what we take the action to be. What our man wants to do is not X *simpliciter*—raising his arm, driving, etc.—but *X-in-the-given-circumstances*, namely, Y—preserving his life. The force of this can be brought out by considering the way in which stating the man's intention is stating his reason for doing what he does. Why does he raise his arm? In order to make a turn. Why does he make a turn? In order to obey his kidnapper. Why do that? In order to preserve his life—he will be killed if he does not obey. The answer to each question makes clear the intention of the agent. In each case it provides us with a further characterization of what the person is doing—he is signalling, obeying orders, preserving his life, and thus getting something he prizes. In making clear what the agent is doing, each answer given makes clear the agent's reason for doing what he does. And it does this by showing us what it is that he wants. Generally, the statement of a man's intentions, by enabling us to understand what he is doing, will enable us to understand what it is that he wants. That it does this depends upon our background understanding of human beings—in our case, the knowledge we have that, in general, they want to preserve their lives.

Further, knowing a man's intention will often enable us to understand why it is that he wants the thing he wants. If, for example, I tell the clerk that I want a pair of shoes with buttons instead of laces, the question, 'Why do you want such shoes?' could be answered by stating the use to which I intend to put them. For example, I intend to use them when I play such-and-such a rôle on the stage. Clearly, explaining my desire, the fact that I want such shoes is the farthest removed from anything like a causal explanation. It is, rather, *making sense of* my desire, by making clear my own status as an actor and hence the sort of thing which I would do with the things.

More obvious perhaps is the case in which saying what a person wants explains what he is doing. Such explanations are sometimes called for when there is calculation involved in a person's conduct and where not all of the relevant circumstances are open to view. For example, if we see someone stop his car on the highway and walk about in the open field examining the ground carefully, 'What does he want?' expresses our inability to understand what he is doing in doing these things. If we are told that he wants to purchase farmland, that will render his conduct intelligible. In walking about, he is getting what he wants in order to decide whether or not this land is desirable, namely, information about the soil. Here the explanation of a man's conduct in terms of his desire turns out to be an explanation of conduct in terms of his intention which gives us an account both of the man—his interests and hence the good with which he is concerned —and of his conduct. Sometimes such explanations are called for when there is no calculation or practical reasoning but when a man clearly is getting something he wants. Why, for example, does a man go about picking up bits of paper? He may, of course, want money; this is how he earns it—he is a scavenger. Or he wants to find a scrap of paper on which he had noted some information and which he had thrown away inadvertently. In general, explaining a man's conduct in all of these cases involves making clear the intention of the agent in doing what he does and hence providing a fuller understanding of his conduct. 'What does he want?' and 'Why does he . . .?' when asked about a man's conduct are two ways of getting at the same thing.

Are there not cases, however, in which a man is the helpless victim of his desires, where there is no calculation or reasoning involved at all and in which a man is moved not by the good in the thing he wants but by the urgency of desire itself? And if there are such cases, desire would appear to be a cause of what is done.

No doubt there are cases in which a man is helpless, *e.g.* the alcoholic who craves drink or the man on the desert who desperately needs water. But where the man is helpless, as indeed he is in these extreme cases, we do not say that he desires or wants but rather that he craves the thing in question. This is no mere linguistic accident. Even if our vocabulary lacked such a word as 'crave', in order to distinguish these cases from the ones we have been examining, we should be led by our interests in conduct to employ some other way of marking off these extreme cases from those in which practical knowledge and deliberation may be involved in conduct. For we are not only concerned to know what is true about persons, what in fact they are doing, we are also interested in helping them, in fixing the proper measures of responsibility, in appraising their conduct as blameworthy, excusable or as exempt from moral or other criticism. The fact that a man may be the helpless victim of a craving for drink, as in the case of the alcoholic, shows *not* that wanting is a cause of his doing, but that he is not responsible for what he does. Even *he* knows what he is doing but not by observation of bodily movements that take place; even *he* has an intention in moving his limbs as he does when he reaches for the drink he cannot resist; even *he* seeks the relief from the tensions he experiences; and so on. And to none of these is the Humean model of causality applicable. His trouble is, rather, that he is ill. Given his condition and the drink before him, he cannot *want* sobriety and all that this makes possible. At best these might appear to be good things to have ('How nice it would be if like others I could enjoy the things they do as sober persons!'); but the sobriety which a non-alcoholic wants and because of which he abstains from the bottle is not a matter with which the alcoholic is or can be similarly concerned. The man who thinks that it would be a good idea to stop smoking has no intention, so far, of doing so, and if this is all that is involved he does not want to stop smoking. The alcoholic may recognize the evils of his condition, he may recognize the desirability of sobriety, but he cannot want sobriety merely by saying 'I want to be sober'. The familiar view is that the alcoholic struggles with two concurrent desires, one for drink, the other for sobriety, and that the former in the contending clash of desires emerges the victor and issues in action. The truth is that much as the alcoholic may wish to refrain from drink he cannot avoid wanting it when he thinks of it; it is not that he wants sobriety but cannot bring himself to secure it, it is rather that in his case the so-called desire for sobriety is really an occasional and idle 'How I wish I were sober!'

But what can the difference be between an idle wish, the mere thought of how nice it would be if . . ., and wanting the thing in question, if it is not that wanting is some moving force that issues in action? Here we need to remind ourselves that the problem of explaining the concept of wanting is not that of explaining how it is that actions are produced. Our starting point is an agent who acts as he does for reasons, because of the desires he has; and our task is to explain not how these actions, fully understood as the actions they are, are produced, but rather how these same actions (so too with the person who performs them) can be more fully understood as the actions they are in fact. Further, our task is not to explain why it is that alcoholics and drug addicts cannot want the things that normal intelligent men want and try to get, but what the connection is between wanting and doing in the case of men who can and do want the things they consider desirable. There could no more be cases of irrational and abnormal action unless there are the familiar cases of intelligent and responsible action, than there could be action that is done without attention and for no reason at all, unless there is action in which an agent is attending to what he is doing and doing it for a reason. We should not even have the concept of an irresponsible, unintelligent, inattentive action unless there were responsible intelligent and attentive actions, just as we should not even have the concept of lying unless there were actual cases of truthtelling. The concept of an action which we have derives from our own status as intelligent, attentive, and responsible agents—this is the logical substratum upon which our concept of an action is based. It is then by reference to features in this sort of case that the connection between wanting and doing must be made out.

Now a man may want something but not even try to get it just as a man may have an idle wish for something but do nothing about getting the object of his wish. But even though neither may do anything, there yet remains a considerable difference between these cases. I am not thinking of the fact that in wanting, the reasonable man believes that there is the thing he wants, and that he has at least the hope of being able to get it—circumstances which certainly do not apply in the case of an idle wish. Rather, I am concerned with the fact that a man who wants an object, whether or not he has deliberated and decided that he wants it, wants to do whatever is required in order to obtain it; whereas a man who entertains an idle wish does not. And if the man who wants sees that he can get the object wanted but does not do anything to get it, the question 'Why don't you get it?' is always intelligible, but the answer 'No reason at all' is always out of order. For if he wants, sees that he can get, but does nothing to get the thing wanted, it follows that he refrains from getting or trying to get the thing wanted; and he refrains from doing so for a reason—he has decided at the very least that the object wanted is not worth all of the bother involved in getting it. But a man with an idle wish, who can but does not do anything to obtain the object of the wish, fails to do anything simply because he does not want it. It is the mark of wanting that in the appropriate circumstances there will be doing, failing which an explanation of the failure to do—which is no mere inactivity but an abstention—is always in order. The man who wants, who has not changed his mind, who sees that he can do something to get the thing wanted, but does nothing, has decided on some ground not to do; no decision of this sort enters into the case of the idle wish. And someone who decides not to do anything about getting what he wants does so because, in the circumstances in which he is placed and to which he attends, doing something would be doing something he does not want to do—at the very least it would be a case of too much bother. No such uses of intelligence need enter into the case of the wish—here one need only reflect upon the agreeable features of having the object of the wish.

But surely 'intention' and 'desire' although related, so I have indicated, are hardly synonymous. I do X (an intentional action) in order to do Y, Y in order to do Z, which I want to do for whatever reason I may have. Granted that in appropriate circumstances the statement of the intention in doing X or Y will make clear what it is that I want—granted too that what I want, in appropriate circumstances, will explain my intention in doing X or Y or Z—still my intentions in doing X, Y or Z are one thing, my desire is something else again. Stating my intentions will fill in details that differ from those filled in by my statement of my desire. And if so, the desire would seem to be a most puzzling event in the proceedings, something different from my intentions in doing X, Y or Z, something which surely can be described as an event and which moves me to act as I do when I do X in order to do Y, Y in order to do Z, and Z in order to get the thing wanted.

No doubt I am moved by my desire and no doubt my desire is an event—something dated. But how am I moved by the desire I now have? The supposition that a desire is some sort of Humean or natural cause will not do. Are we obliged then to resort to indefinables, to positing some *sui generis* type of causation? But this, all other reasons apart, leaves us with the mystery of mental events—desires—whose character has suddenly become impossibly elusive. If I say that I want X because of the occurrence of this event, the event cannot be elusive, hidden—it must be transparently clear. And, as Wittgenstein remarked in another connection, how if it is hidden will I recognize it if and when I do find it?

In order to dispel the threatening mystery, let us reconsider the point made earlier that if someone stops his car and is asked 'Why?', the statement 'There is a restaurant nearby' is not to be understood merely as a bit of information but as *a reason for the action*. It is one thing to play the game of reporting one's observations, it is quite another thing to give reasons for one's conduct. To see this, compare the reasoning of one preparing to stop for food with one who simply

160

remarks upon the places he sees. In the latter case, it would not be logically incoherent or even puzzling for someone to say 'There is a restaurant nearby where food can be obtained, but I don't want any'. But in the former case the practical reasoning is 'There is a restaurant nearby where food can be obtained, so I'll stop'; to add to the reasons given for stopping 'But I don't want any' *is* queer. One can of course imagine a case in which this is intelligible—the speaker is making it clear that what he wants is not food but something else one can get in places where food is obtainable—he may have the strange hobby of collecting menus just as some people collect postage stamps or even theatre-tickets. Or perhaps it is not that he wants food but that the person sitting beside him does, given which, it follows logically from the fact that 'There is a restaurant nearby where food is obtainable' announces a reason for his stopping the car, that he wants to enable the other person to get the food he wants. It is then no accident that stating a reason for doing is making clear what it is that is wanted. And if one's reason for stopping is *simply* that there is a restaurant nearby where food can be obtained, adding 'I want food' is not adding a *further* reason one has for stopping but making it clear that there is no further reason to be given. So too, adding 'I don't want food' can only serve to specify that the announced reason is not the whole story of the reasons to be given—that one is stopping, not in order to get food but something else, or, if it is food that is wanted, it is not by the agent but by someone else whose want or desire the agent wants to satisfy. But apart from such uses as these, 'I want . . .', and 'I don't want . . .'

161

can serve no linguistic function as mere *additions* to our familiar statements of our reasons for acting—in the first case because 'I want . . .' would be a uselessly dangling verbal appendage, in the latter case because it would give rise to incoherence. *Wanting enters into our practical reasoning not as a premise (i.e. 'I want . . .' is not itself a reason over and above the reasons I can and do give), but into our understanding of the premises which we offer as our reasons for our doings.*

But how does the wanting enter into the thinking, into the *understanding*, of the reasons given for the action? Certainly 'There is a restaurant nearby' is true, and how can one event—wanting—'enter into' (and in what sense?) another event logically distinct from it —the recognition of this truth? Surely this is a mystifying way of speaking! But if there is mystery here, it is of our own making. For viewed this way, we do have something incomprehensible—a logically internal relation between logically independent events—for of course one can want but not recognize the truth, or, recognize the truth but not want. But here the trouble is the vexingly persistent contemplative view of reason —the idea that it is the primary function of reason to recognize matters of fact—to pick out objects, their qualities and their relations. Now it is no coincidence that I have insisted that our starting point in our account of action and related concepts is that of an agent who knows his way about in his traffic with the persons and the objects about him. For the force of this insistence is to weaken the effective hold upon our imaginations of the conception of a person contemplating objects and recognizing or picking out the truths about them. Here we need to be reminded that the concept of a reason for action, like the concepts of intention, action and desire, are practical concepts, that they are concepts employed by us in our intelligent responses to and dealings with the things about us. It is not, then, that an agent experiences one event —the itch or twitch of desire—and another—the experience of objects whose qualities or relations he contemplates. If this were so, how would he connect the desire with the thing he contemplates—the food he sees before him with the desire the former enables him to satisfy? Would he not require inductive evidence for the belief that it is food that he desires, that getting and eating the food would satisfy the desire whether or not he, in getting and eating it, would be satisfied? But we do not have two events, the desire, and the apprehension of the fact that here there is food, plus some belief, whose rational basis is at best problematic, that the former—the desire—is a desire for the latter—the food. On the contrary, our starting point is the case of an agent whose intelligence is exhibited in his dealings with the food before him. Viewed in this way, the food before him is no mere blend of carbohydrates, proteins and fats, no mere rounded slab of brownish or blackened fibrous material, which has been sliced off from the carcass of a steer and is now sizzling on the platter before him. It is, rather, a steak, *i.e.* something to be relished in the eating, an object with which a person can do something and in the doing of which he exhibits both his desires and the manner in which he views or grasps what is before him.

What we must do, therefore, is to recover our every-

day sense that the objects about us are things to be
dealt with in the various ways in which this is done
by rational and volitional creatures. The food before
me is something to be eaten, the restaurant nearby is
a place where we can obtain it. One can, of course,
adopt a relatively pallidly neutral view of both—
neutral with respect to the human desire for food.
One can regard food as a peculiar complex of organic
materials, and one can regard the restaurant nearby
as a business establishment that plays an economic
rôle in the economic life of the community. But these
are sophisticated performances in which one can
engage precisely because we have already learned how
to recognize these in the everyday way in which people
do when they want food and get what they want in
restaurants that serve them. What we need to do,
therefore, is to recover our sense of the character of
our experience of and our thinking about the things
we want, *because* we want them. But here the *because*
marks not the occurrence of an event that produces
such experiences and thinking, but rather their
character. Wanting something involves thinking about
it in a different way—thinking about the object as
something with which the agent is to do something;
and if the object is before one, wanting it involves
seeing it as something with which this doing is to be
performed. But it is not enough that one thinks about
the object as something with which some doing can
be performed—this can happen when one does not
want it. Nor is it enough that I see it as something with
which I am to do something—for this can happen
when I am ordered to do but want neither the object
nor anything to do with it. Here we need to be re-

minded of our earlier remarks about the sorts of experiences one may have when one does something intentionally. These experiences vary from situation to situation. So too in the case of wanting. There is no single nuclear experience of wanting. And here we need to look ingenuously not only at the variety of feelings—the urges, the impulses, the tensions, the way in which one thinks with relish and even sometimes with discomfort about diverse matters at hand, but the circumstances in which these occur—the actions that follow or the restraints one imposes upon oneself in consequence of one's decision not to get what one wants, etc., etc. We need to consider, in short, the various ways in which, to use a very broad term, our experiences are patterned within the context of actions or abstentions in varying circumstances in which one finds oneself, when one wants something and either does or refrains from doing. It is, then, understandable that there should be those borderline cases in which a man, through lack of perspicacity about himself, may not be aware of some of the desires he has which explain his otherwise puzzling or aberrant behaviour.

But surely one can understand that 'There is a restaurant nearby where food is obtainable' is a reason for going there without actually having the desire for food! Certainly, one can also understand that something amusing occurred without being amused by the thought, or that a poem is beautiful without sharing the experiences of one who appreciates the aesthetic qualities of the poem. But it would be impossible to understand that a poem was beautiful if one were devoid of aesthetic taste—if one never appreciated the aesthetic qualities of a poem. It would be impossible for one without a sense of humour—one who was never amused—to understand the remark that something was amusing. And a pure intelligence —if one could think of such a thing—which lacked the experience of one who sees something called 'food' as something to be eaten, which was incapable of thinking about that kind of object as something to be relished or avoided, to be regarded with the feelings—the tensions, urges, impulses, etc., of one who does want food, and gets or decides for one reason or another not to get it—such a being simply would not understand 'There is a restaurant nearby where food is obtainable' in the way in which we do when we recognize that it is a reason for doing. One's wanting is something that happens—a mental event if one pleases—but it is an event that consists in the occurrence of these familiar incidents of our lives that vary in diverse ways in different circumstances.

I have argued in these last chapters that the connection between wanting and doing is logical, not causal in the Humean or familiar sense in which this term is employed in the natural sciences. What a man does, when he wants, is therefore no evidence for his wanting in the way in which red spots on the skin are evidence of measles; doing is no symptom of some inner activity of wanting. It is at least conceivable that a man should have the disease but give no indication, show no symptoms. So one could understand a description of a disease—the presence of certain minute organisms in the body—which would not involve any reference to the normal effect, namely, the red spots on the skin. But it is not possible to

166

understand the language of wanting or desiring from which all references to doing have been stripped. A 'pure' language of wanting from which all reference to doing has been removed is as impossible as a language of 'pure sensation'. Nor is it the case that our concept of wanting can be grasped if we ignore the logical connections of this concept with those of the desirable, decision, reason, hope, belief, and so on. These related concepts provide the logical scaffolding which fixes the position of 'wanting' in our language.

Yet 'wanting' can be applied to animals even though some of the above-mentioned concepts have no application in the explanation of their behaviour, just because there is some similarity between the actions of human beings and animals. Refraining from getting what one wants, *i.e.* deciding not to get what one wants, is after all a learned and sophisticated performance when it is dictated by considerations of the undesirability of doing so. 'Wanting', then, like 'doing', is applied to animals and to infants in a truncated manner—some of the features of our very rich concept of wanting have no application in these cases. But if we want to understand what wanting is we shall have to understand the unsophisticated incidents in the lives of animals and very young children to which, albeit in a truncated way, this concept is applicable. In other words, we shall need to look to the spontaneous, natural cases in which wanting explains doing and in which, unlike the full-blown cases of intelligent and responsible human beings, there is nothing like the restraint or abstention from doing for various sorts of reasons.

This situation is in an important respect like the

case of understanding propositions about sensations. In Chapter IV, I remarked that descriptions of sensations are logically derivative from the descriptions we first learn to apply to objects; the philosophical view that we first learn to describe sensations and then apply such descriptions to objects reverses the logical order. We learn first to describe objects in our practical dealings with them; only then is it logically possible to offer the sophisticated descriptions of our sensations. If, then, we are to understand the logical features of the accounts we give about our sensations, we must understand the unsophisticated ways in which we apply descriptive terms to objects about us. So although our concept of 'red' is an enriched concept which we apply both to objects and to our sensations, we need, in order to grasp it, to see how it is employed in the first-learned and unsophisticated accounts given by the child of the objects it touches and handles. This is the analogy between propositions about sensations and propositions about intentions and wanting which Wittgenstein drew:

'What is the natural expression of an intention?— Look at a cat when it stalks a bird; or a beast when it wants to escape.

((Connection with propositions about sensations.))'[1] Just as we need, in order to understand propositions about sensations, to look to the ways in which descriptive terms are employed in the unsophisticated, first-learned, descriptions of objects, so we need, in order to understand propositions about wanting, to look to the ways in which animals, uninhibited and unsophisticated and oblivious to the sorts of reasons that

[1] *Philosophical Investigations*, §647.

explain abstentions, calculated and even devious actions, try to get or succeed in getting what they want. It is by reference to such doings that the rudiments of the concept of wanting can be grasped, for here the wanting is exhibited transparently in the very character of the doing itself and in the elementary intelligence of the agent—of a cat that sees a bird as something to be eaten, of a beast that understands a trap only as something that prevents it from doing what it wants to do, of an infant that sees a rattle, not as a plastic toy (for it has no contrasting concept to employ) but as a shiny thing to be put in its mouth.

In this connection it is worth commenting upon the term 'criterion' which Wittgenstein uses in a way that contrasts with the way in which we speak of red spots on the skin as a symptom or indication of the presence of measles. When a man raises his arm, because he wants something (saying what he wants will generally make clear the intention he has in raising his arm), he not only raises his arm but also reaches for what he wants. Saying what he wants, then, is explaining what he is doing—he is reaching for what he wants. Yet there are not two distinct events, one the action of raising his arm, the other the action of reaching for what he wants, in the way in which raising one's arm (in signalling) is one thing and pressing the brake-pedal is another. Raising his arm, then, is not evidence for his reaching for what he wants in the way in which red spots are evidence for or a symptom of measles, for it is the same event that can be described both as the action of raising his arm and the action of reaching for what he wants. *A fortiori* raising his arm is not evidence for, or a symptom of, his wanting. But, in

169

appropriate circumstances, the raising of the arm is understood correctly as a case of reaching for what is wanted. Reaching for what is wanted (trying to get, getting what one wants) logically implies wanting. To mark the way in which the case of raising the arm can be the very same thing as a case of wanting, the term 'criterion' is usefully employed. Thus a criterion of a man's wanting is his doing, *e.g.* raising his arm, not because this doing *so described* logically implies that there is wanting, nor that this doing is a necessary condition, causal or otherwise, of his wanting (for a man may want but not do, as we have seen) but because in appropriate circumstances this doing is intelligible only as a doing that one performs when one wants. It is this sort of logical relation that the term 'criterion' is designed to mark.

CHAPTER THIRTEEN

BODILY MOVEMENT, ACTION
AND AGENT

IT will be useful at this time to bring together the tangled threads of the argument. It will be remembered that I reviewed a number of attempts to explain the distinction between a bodily movement or happening and a bodily action, in terms of the order of causes. I concluded that it is impossible by any adjunction of events or factors to transform a bodily movement into an item of human action. This moral has now been reinforced by the detailed inquiry into the rôle of motives and desires in the explanation of human conduct. Traditionally, these have been construed as causal factors, internal thrusts or pushes that issue in movements or actions, the distinction between which has been generally obscured by the muddying term 'overt behaviour'. But the connection between these and action is, I argued, a logical connection, not causal. It is impossible to grasp the concepts of motive and desire independently of the concept of an action. And, further, the sense in which a motive or a desire explains an item of conduct is altogether different from the sense in which, say, the presence of a spark explains the explosion of a mixture of petrol vapour

171

and air. Our concern with matters of conduct, in inquiring into a man's motive or desire, is not to discover whether a case of a bodily movement is a case of an action—that much is already settled in our minds when we ask what a person's motive is or what it is that he desires—nor is it to discover how it is that a case of a bodily movement, now understood as an action, has been produced. Our concern, rather, is to learn something more about the character of both the man and his action.

But how does all of this contribute to an understanding of the concept of an action, as distinguished from that of a mere bodily movement? And if, as I argued in the preceding chapter, our starting point in the explanation of the rôle of intentions and desires in conduct is a human agent, a being who acts intelligently, attentively and for a reason, does this not imply that the concepts of agent and action are primitive and indefinable? In that case the obscurantism in the intuitionist's account of acts of volition has indeed come home to roost, albeit on a different perch.

These are related questions but disturbing as they may appear on first sight, the results so far achieved in the account of both intentions and desires are of major importance in removing their sting.

To begin with, a necessary comment about philosophical explanation, in particular the sort of explanation given of the concepts of intention and desire in the preceding chapters. For reasons I have indicated, it is natural to suppose that the difficulty we may have in understanding what an intention or desire is, is the difficulty involved in the discovery of an elusive item in our experience. We intend and desire; and because we do, we act. Intentions and desires, being dated, are phenomena of our inner experiences; hence they are causal factors that normally issue in conduct. But pictured in this way, they become mysterious indeed. What are the events that occur whenever, and only when, we intend or desire something? And how can such events, supposing there were any, exhibit the required logical features of intentions and desires? The task of giving a proper account of these matters by discovering the properties of events labelled 'intentions' and 'desires' is not simply difficult because of the elusiveness of the events in question; it is, rather, hopelessly impossible. This sort of move is a familiar one in philosophy. It arises quite naturally in the puzzles and obscurities that surround the concept of meaning—the elusive mental processes that ride piggy-back, so to speak, on the words we utter and which, allegedly, constitute our understanding of them. So it is in the case of promises: since one cannot bind one-self simply by uttering words, the promise must consist therefore in something mental in which we engage when we utter the words 'I promise . . .'. But the elusiveness of these alleged processes derives from the fact that no event distinguishable from the uttering of the words, either in the case of the promise or in that of meaning, exhibits the required logical features.[1] In these as well as in other cases the difficulty we encounter, as Wittgenstein has remarked, seems at first sight to be that of attempting to discover something

[1] It is interesting that Hume was led, on account of the difficulty, nay the impossibility, of accounting for the commonly ascribed property of a promise that it obliges, to appeal to a 'feigning of the imagination', a bizarre fiction that could not conceivably be true. Cf. my paper 'On Promising' in *Mind*, January 1956.

that eludes our ordinary view of what goes on in our minds, as if we could, by a more critical inspection, by adjusting the focus of our intellectual microscopes (this is his figure of speech), bring into view the hidden event that slips by too quickly and thus eludes our coarser inspection. But this is an enormous paradox, for how if this were so would it be possible for persons of quite ordinary intelligence and perspicacity to employ as they do the concepts in question?

But this, it may be charged, is unfair. Our business as philosophers is, as it is often put, to analyse concepts, not to make quasi-empirical discoveries of events and their properties. But how does one 'analyse' a concept? No doubt there are complex features of concepts like those of intention and desire—this indeed is what I attempted to show in the preceding chapters. But does this mean that a concept is some sort of refined complex of parts, the composition of which escapes us, as indeed the composition of sugar now escapes me? And if by 'analysing a concept' one does not intend the sort of logical decomposition into constituents with which Moore, for example, believed himself to be concerned in *Principia Ethica*, what does 'analysing a concept' mean? The truth is that the term 'analysis' is very often a bit of jargon, frequently applied as a term of conceit to anything one says about any subject at all, however vague, muddled and intellectually irresponsible one's talk may be. In any case, what are the concepts with which we are concerned when, as philosophers, we address ourselves to intentions, desires and the like? The trouble here is that the expression 'analysis of concepts' often conceals and embodies a crucial philosophical prepossession. We are led to look for the elusive hidden events to which we attach the labels 'intention', 'desire', 'meaning', 'promise', etc., *thus* converting a question about meaning into an extremely questionable view about matters of psychological occurrence (this indeed is the fatal blunder), because of the picture commonly conveyed by the term 'concept'. We suppose, for reasons I have been at pains to express and expose, that our concepts of intention and desire, like the others I have cited above, are the concepts of happenings that could conceivably operate in the mechanism of a mind; and hence that an account of these concepts would consist in setting forth a list of properties that could be ascribed to the happenings properly labelled by the terms 'intention' and 'desire'. This, as we have seen, is to lead us down the garden path; no such events are discoverable precisely because no such events could exhibit the requisite logical features of the concepts *we* employ.

What we need to do, therefore, is to abandon this picture and instead to examine carefully the manner in which terms like 'intention' and 'desire' operate in our familiar discourse about actions and agents. There is no royal road to the understanding of these and other related concepts by some sort of sheer intuition of non-temporal objects of the mind—entities labelled 'concepts' whose complex constitution it is our business as philosophers to lay bare. And if we suppose that entities of this kind are the subject of our inquiry, then here too questions of meaning are transformed illegitimately into questions of discovery: the disclaimers by some philosophers that they are unable to intuit the alleged objects must be put down to the paradoxical fact that these philosophers, who after all do show a grasp of the concepts in their familiar use of these terms, lack the required ability to perform an act of critical inspection; or worse, that they are dishonest. But even if we granted the existence of certain objects of intellection, the test of a person's understanding would remain, as always, his grasp of the manner in which the words 'intention' and 'desire' are employed in our discourse about agents and their actions. Understanding consists, indeed, in understanding the import of statements about intentions and desires by recognizing, *among other things*, the relevance to such statements of the various forms of questions that may be raised and the answers that may be given, the challenges that may be made and the manner in which they may be met. In short, it would consist in understanding the character of the language in which these terms and their cognates are embedded, and thereby the crucial logical relations between these and other concepts.

It is this view of the matter that the tediously detailed inquiry in the preceding chapters has been designed to promote. We have seen something of the complexity involved in the understanding of the concepts that concern us by exploring certain of the logical relations that hold between the concepts of intention, desire, action, agent, reason for acting, the desirable, belief, hope and decision. It is no accident that in our account of desires we have been led back to the concept of intention, to recognize that one may explain an agent's conduct equally well by making clear what it is that he wants as by stating what it is that he intends in acting as he does. For a statement of intention, insofar as it is a declaration of a man's reasons for doing what he does, does this precisely because there is something to be got by his action which he wants and if his reasons justify him in his conduct, some envisaged good to be achieved thereby. Yet 'intention' and 'desire' are no mere synonyms even though in practical circumstances 'what does he want?' and 'why does he do . . .?' when asked about a man's conduct are only different ways of getting at the same thing—a better understanding of both a man's conduct and his interests—by calling for the filling in of different but related details in the proceedings we want to understand.

Our account of the place of intentions and desires in the conceptual framework of our language must necessarily be incomplete. A full account would call for a detailed examination of notions like choice, deliberation, expectation, belief, decision and the like —a whole gamut of mental terms which have figured importantly in the debates pro and con the possibility of free and responsible action. To do this would be an enormous task: it would consist in tracing out the complex conceptual pattern embodied in our total discourse about persons and their conduct, including a detailed examination of the whole cluster of related concepts involved in the notion of a reason for doing. I have connected this idea with that of something wanted by the agent who can and does want things for the good in them. That there is a restaurant across the street, for example, may be interesting and true, but this does not justify his crossing the street unless there is something he wants and can get there, *e.g.* food, which is worth having. But there is neither a single good to be achieved by all action nor is there always a single way in which any good may be secured. 'Good' is by no means the exclusive preserve of moralists. It would be excessive moralism to make a moral issue in general about getting such goods as pleasure, health or aesthetic satisfaction, just as it would be ridiculous if not indecent to argue for the morality of one's conduct by appealing to the pleasure it affords, the health it promotes or the aesthetic satisfactions it provides. That pleasure is good is a tautology, and so with health and aesthetic appreciation. But any good, moral or not, may be secured in indefinitely many ways. Consider the very many ways in which a person's reason for doing something may be involved in getting food for the good, namely health, that it provides; and consider all of the very many sorts of things a person may do merely in order to get proper food. He will perhaps be guided by the advice of his physician or follow his orders. Or, he will purchase food and in doing so exchange money for food, thus participating in a transaction intelligible only in the light of an elaborate system or conventions and statutes—for there is a difference between placing coloured pieces of paper in the palm of a person's hand and making a payment to a grocer for food received; yet paying a grocer is no less an action, something one can observe taking place, than moving a piece of coloured paper from here to there by executing the required and in itself complicated bodily action. Or, one will drive one's car to the market in order to get food; yet think of the very many sorts of bodily actions one will perform in the course of doing this and how, *e.g.* raising one's arm, given the rules of the road, and the proper circumstances, is the action of signalling. And one can get the proper food by stealing it from the grocer, yet it would be ridiculous to attempt to justify the theft on the ground that one was following doctor's orders even if the doctor had ordered one to eat that kind of food. So there are moral considerations variously described by writers as rules, principles, precepts or maxims, to be observed in one's doings, all of which may also be described as getting food that is good for one. One could go on, too, to remark upon other social matters and conventions: the expectations of others which we take account of in our conduct and our expectations of their conduct to which we adjust in acting as we do; our abstentions in order to permit or to allow others to act and conversely (as in the case of a motorist who waits for pedestrians to cross the road before he proceeds); the matters of small manners (but how important when ignored or flouted!) that normally govern even trivial cases of social intercourse; and so on indefinitely.

All this is not to say that one could not have a conception of a human action unless one had the conception of traffic rules, or of these particular rules, laws or conventions governing the social intercourse of persons which happen to obtain in our society at this or that particular time. But if we are concerned with action we are concerned with the actions of human beings who are social and moral beings and who are guided in their conduct by social and moral considerations in their dealings with one another. Nor is it necessary if, correctly, we apply the term 'action' to an observed motion of someone's arm, that it must be possible to describe in social and moral terms what the person is doing. There may be no reason of any sort applicable to a given case; to 'Why?' the correct answer may be, 'No reason at all'. And even if a reason may be given, that reason need not involve any matter of social or moral import: 'Why did you raise your arm?'—'To stretch my muscles.' Yet to understand the concept of a human action we need to understand the *possibilities* of descriptions in social and moral terms; we need to recognize, in other words, the relevance and applicability of reasons that operate, not only in the privacy of one's study, but also in the social arena where persons take account of each other in doing what they do and are guided in their thought and action by an intricate network of moral and social considerations.

In earlier chapters I explored some of the conceptual connections between action, desire, intention, belief, etc. In the present chapter I remarked that this marks only the beginning of the investigation of the network of concepts which needs to be carried forward in order to understand the conceptual rôle of the term 'action' in our language. But it is clear now that we need also to focus attention upon the very many descriptions of actions which follow logically from the correspondingly many sorts of reasons for actions noted above and, in addition, the goods with which human beings are concerned. But this is to say that no account of the concept of action will do that does not attend to the status of a person as a practical being, one who is not only endowed with the primitive ability to move his limbs but who, in his complex dealings with others, acts as he does for the very many sorts of reasons that operate in conduct and out of concern with a variety of envisaged goods. 'Action' and 'agent' are conceptually related terms, not only in the anaemic sense that where there is action there is agent, and conversely, but more importantly because the character of the conception of the one is logically connected with the character of our conception of the other. And since our conception of an action is not restricted to that of a bodily action but applies to bodily actions and abstentions which are understood as cases of dealings—more or less complex in respect of the background against which they must be viewed in order to be understood—of social and moral beings with one another, the concept of a person must also be enlarged and enriched. For a person is no mere owner of mental status, no mere mover of arms and legs, but a being who has such states and does such things in the very many sorts of transactions in which he engages, not only with the things that interest and concern him in the privacy of his study but also with the persons to whose interests, actions, hopes, etc., he is attentive in the conduct of his life.

In the previous chapter I argued that if we are to understand the concepts with which we are concerned in this inquiry, our starting point must be that of an agent who acts, one who does things for a reason and with proper attention to what he is about. Failure to adopt this correct starting point is the source of the recurrent appeal in the history of philosophy to a mysterious efficacy or power ascribable to agents or persons and in terms of which allegedly the notion of a human action is to be viewed. It is unnecessary to comment upon the inherent obscurity of such a move

—a typical appeal to indefinables that makes a mystery of the most commonplace matter. But this recently revived move does have a point. It is in fact the point which Hume in his attack on the idea of causal efficacy failed completely to recognize; and the fact that his own version of causation may not do justice to the sorts of explanations of events provided in well-established physical sciences adds more than a touch of irony to the history of the debate. For the alleged idea of causal efficacy or power by which events, according to its proponents, are necessitated is an idea that has always been thought to be peculiarly relevant to the actions of agents. The fact that the philosophers Hume attacked applied this obscure notion of agency to all natural phenomena and thus lent cogency to his polemic obscured what was important in the idea of causal efficacy—something Hume simply failed to recognize, namely, that an action is no mere effect of an internal mental doing in the way in which an explosion is an effect of the introduction of heat in a mixture of hydrogen and oxygen. Contemporary writers who have revived this talk about powers and agencies do not, in general, wish to apply this way of speaking to natural phenomena; they restrict it to agents and their actions. It is no good, except as a first step, attacking this move on the grounds of its inherent obscurity. What is important is, first, to recognize the legitimacy of the consideration that prompts this philosophically stultifying move, namely, the inapplicability of the ordinary causal model to the scene of human action, and secondly, the mistake of supposing that because ordinary causal models will not fit—for actions are no mere happenings, and it is *persons* that act—some mysterious, elusive causal power of a higher order is needed. Philosophers who invoke such powers have succumbed to the fascination of the causal model of explanation. And it is this appeal to indefinables which our starting point—agents acting attentively and for reasons—is designed to preclude.

But how does our starting point—the fact that a person attends to what he is doing and acts as he does for reasons of one sort or another—enable us to explain the concept of an action? How in particular does this enable us to grasp the distinction between a bodily movement and an action, *e.g.* the distinction between the rising of one's arm and the action of raising one's arm? And how does it enable us to avoid the conclusion that the notions of action and agent are somehow primitive, to be taken for granted but not themselves the subject of further explanation?

But the outline of the answer to the first question, and by implication to the second, should now be clear. By adopting our procedure we have seen something of the character of the concepts we employ in our familiar everyday explanations of conduct. I have remarked that this is only the beginning of an inquiry that needs to take into account other concepts like those of decision, choice, deliberation and so on which together with the concepts examined constitute the vast and complicated conceptual network embedded in the discourse that is applicable to human action. And, further, in examining the notions of reasons for acting, including justifications for doing, and hence of goods with which agents are concerned, I have commented upon the enormous complexity of considerations, attention to which is required in order to recognize the character of the discourse relevant and applicable to persons and their actions. In short, our inquiry has emphasized what is crucial to an understanding of actions and agents and what is easily neglected if we focus our attention upon what happens at the time an agent does anything, namely, the logical character of the language we apply to actions, in contradistinction to that employed by physiologists and others who are concerned with a scientific grasp of the causal circumstances of bodily movements or happenings. Small wonder we turn to occult powers in our account of action when we are struck by the peculiar irrelevance to conduct of the concepts employed by physiologists! Small wonder, too, the incoherences involved in the attempt to explain an action in terms of the order of causes of the bodily movement—acts of volitions or any other alleged causal factors—or by conjoining bodily movement or happening with any other event in the alleged mechanism of the mind or of the body! Where we are concerned with causal explanations, with events of which the happenings in question are effects in accordance with some law of causality, to that extent we are not concerned with human actions at all but, at best, with bodily movements or happenings; and where we are concerned with explanations of human action, there causal factors and causal laws in the sense in which, for example, these terms are employed in the biological sciences are wholly irrelevant to the understanding we seek. The reason is simple, namely, the radically different logical characteristics of the two bodies of discourse we employ in these distinct cases—the different concepts which are applicable to these different orders of inquiry.

Suppose we observe some bodily movement—a person's arm is rising in the air. Considered simply *as* a bodily movement it is an event wholly explicable in terms of the movements of the muscles on the skeleton of the arm. If need be, the matter may be explored further by investigating the detailed way in which the stimuli applied to muscle fibres result in their contraction and relaxation in the manner in which this happens when the arm rises in the air. And, further, one could go on to inquire about the functions of the nervous system and the neurological conditions of the transmission of stimuli from the brain to the muscle-fibres of the arm. In this context of inquiry it is senseless to ask 'Why?' in any sense in which the question calls for an answer in terms of an agent's intentions, desires, reasons for doing, and so on. Not even 'No reason' is relevant here. For 'No reason' *is* an answer to the question 'Why did you do . . .?', just as 'Nothing' is an answer to the question 'How much did you win?' But where it makes no sense to speak of winning any amount at all, it makes no sense to speak of winning no amount at all; and there it makes no sense to ask how much was won. Just so, in the physiologist's context of inquiry, the 'Why?' that calls for an answer in terms of some reason the agent has for acting, has no place at all. So far, neither action nor agent comes within the scope of the investigation. Here there is no place for any of the descriptions and explanations that are appropriate to human conduct. None of the logically connected concepts embedded in our discourse about action applies to this case.

But just how is it that we can *treat* a case of a bodily movement as a case of an action? There is a Kantian

ring to the suggestion that we apply action concepts
—the concept of an action and those which are logically related to it—to an observed bodily movement. Do
we *interpret* a bodily movement as an action? But how
would we do *that*? And what would count as a correctly
interpreted bodily movement? If we interpreted bodily
movements as actions—*e.g.* the rising of the arm as
the action of raising the arm—it would be necessary
that we have some idea of the sort of considerations
that would justify us in such interpretations. But how
could anything, short of an appeal to what the person
has done or goes on to do, settle the question for us?
And if we ask him whether he *has* raised his arm and
settle the matter in our minds on the basis of what he
tells us then this telling, upon which we rely, is something he does, and no mere movement of vocal chords
that issue in the noises we hear when we attend to
what he says. But if we must interpret *every* bodily
movement as a case of an action, then nothing could
serve to justify any interpretation—everything must
then hang in the air without any conceivable support.
In that case every application of action-concepts to
any proceedings is worse off than the wildest guess—
for when we guess we know how to go on to find out
whether we have hit the mark. In short, it must be
the exception, rather than the general rule, that we
interpret bodily movements as actions; it is no more
thinkable that every bodily movement is so interpreted than that everything we read is infected with
exegesis or surmise as to what the author meant. In
most cases there is no interpretation at all, no reflection, consideration or decision, no exercise of
judgment, no room for hesitation or doubt. We simply

see a person raising his arm just as we read off what we find on the printed page.

But how is it possible for us to *see* a person raise his arm, to *see* a bodily movement as an action? Well, how is it possible for us to read a printed page, to see, not curiously shaped black marks on a white background, but the sentences that lie before us? Here the answer is simply 'Training'. No doubt a person's intellectual faculties are developed when he has learned how to read, for if he reads he does on occasion at least reflect, weigh, deliberate, infer and in various other ways think about the statements of the author; but all of this is consequential to the reading the person has been trained to do. And if it seems odd to say that what a person sees depends upon the training he has received, compare the visual experiences of one who merely looks at the pattern of marks on a printed page with the visual experiences of one who is reading.[1] There is a difference between seeing marks on a page and reading words. So too there is a difference between observing bodily movements and observing actions, *i.e.* seeing bodily movements as cases of actions. Here the activities in which we have been trained to engage in our dealings with one another constitute the substratum upon which our recognition of the actions of others rests. We have then no mere system of abstract concepts of the understanding which we apply to some alien material of experience, but a complex of activi-

[1] Speaking about the case of a triangle in which one can see now *this* as apex and now *that* as base, Wittgenstein remarks, ' "Now he's seeing it like *this*", "now like *that*" would only be said of someone *capable* of making certain applications of the figure quite freely.' And he goes on to remark, 'The substratum of this experience is the mastery of a technique.' *Philosophical Investigations*, p. 208e.

187

ties we have been trained to perform, in the context of which the discourse we employ plays its rôle in communication and by virtue of which we see as we do the bodily movements of others as the actions of persons. It is this training that is of central importance both to our understanding of the concepts of action and agent and to our perception of the actions of those about us.

Consider the infant's action of raising its arm. In an earlier section I referred to the primitive ability which we have of moving our limbs; and I rejected the view that a child learns to do this in the way in which it learns, say, to open a door by turning the knob and pulling on it. Here it makes sense to speak of the infant's raising its arm, for here it makes sense to ask why it does this and to say that it does this either for no reason or in order to reach for the bauble suspended above its head. We thus have in a very rudimentary way something like the starting point upon which I insisted—an agent attentive to what is going on about it and capable of doing what it does for some sort of reason. Learning is possible here but in very important ways it takes the form of training. The recognition or understanding that this very young child has is circumscribed by a set of very rudimentary interests. The bauble is something to play with, the light is something that intrigues or irritates it, the mother is something from which it obtains food and relief from discomfort. It may be that in the case of the very young child, instinctive behaviour and action shade into one another, but where clear-cut actions are performed, our account of them is apt to suffer from an over-sophistication. *We* say that it reaches for a

188

bauble or that it smiles at its mother but the concepts of bauble and mother which *we* employ reflect the interests *we* have and are not those of the infant. For it, the bauble is no material object describable in our familiar way, but a shiny something to be touched and played with; and the mother is no madonna who happily assumes the responsibility of training and guiding it to an increasing participation in the affairs of both the family and society, but something from which it gains its creature comforts and something with which it plays. As yet there is neither recognition of agent nor action in anything that its mother does, for so far there is no discrimination between material object and agent in anything of which it takes account and hence no recognition of its own status as agent.

It is important not only to appreciate the vast gulf that separates the very young child's sense of what goes on about it from the understanding we have—hence James' description of its experience as buzzing, booming and confused—but also to notice the crucial rôle played by training in the increasingly refined discernment it gains as it matures and develops. If it is to recognize its mother as one to be obeyed, training is necessary, including the training involved in recognizing sounds as commands. A being, if one could imagine one, who had not been trained to obey would not understand what obedience is and would not understand the rôle in communication of a command utterance. So it is with those forms of discourse by which one offers sympathy and encouragement, offers and ask for food, plays games and so on. The child needs to be trained to perform the activities in the context of which these utterances play their rôle in communication—in Wittgenstein's technical term, the language-game appropriate to each of these forms of discourse. In short, the child needs to be trained, by participation in the various forms of activity in which it engages with its mother, to recognize *this* bodily movement of its mother in *this* transaction in which it engages as *this* action, *that* bodily movement in *that* transaction as *that* action. Only in the context of the specific activities which it has been trained to perform, as it grows into its changing rôles with respect to its mother and to the other members of the family, is it possible for it to understand the bodily movements of those participating in their diverse ways in the life of the family as the actions they are, and to understand what it is to be a mother, a father, a sister, or a brother. So one could go on to explore the manner in which the concepts of action and agent are enriched by relating to the wider scenes of social intercourse in which in diverse ways various social and moral institutions, conventions, statutes, etc., are relevant to the background activities against which bodily movements are understood as the actions they are and agents as the familiar sorts of persons we understand them to be: employers and employees, sellers and purchasers, motorists, strangers, friends—the list is almost endless.

When we ask why it is that someone is doing what he is doing in raising his arm it may well be that we know what, in a general way, he is up to, and we may be quite well aware of the sort of activity that provides the background against which this bodily movement is to be understood as, say, the action of signalling a turn. He is, we see clearly, driving his car and because of our familiarity with the rules of the road, we recognize well enough that he is signalling. But just as it is impossible for a person to be *merely* a person, so it is impossible for a person to be merely a motorist. A traffic policeman will perhaps consider persons simply as motorists, passengers or pedestrians, as he discharges his duties. But our interest in knowing why the person in question is signalling is not so circumscribed. For the answer to this question which states the motorist's intention—let us say that he does this because he is on his way to the store on the street into which he is about to turn—enables us to understand what the motorist is doing by specifying his further status as a person: he is on his way to make a purchase. Sometimes the question 'Why?' is asked when there is uncertainty in our minds about the relevant activity to be taken into account in understanding both the character of the action and the status of the person: for example, is he raising his arm to signal to the operator of the hoist or to summon assistance in carrying out some task? Sometimes the question is asked when we are fully aware of the general character of the action and the status of the person but do not understand how it is that he hopes to succeed in his task: he is, say, a garage mechanic trying to repair the motor of one's car and tinkers with some lever or gadget. And sometimes we are uncertain about the relevance of *any* activity in which he is engaged or any specific status which he has as a person: Is he raising his arm for no reason at all or is he simply stretching? But we could not have the concept of an action unless we understood what it is to do something for a reason. And we could not have the concept of

191

doing something for a reason unless we had received the sort of training which enables us to engage in various transactions with specific sorts of persons and thus treat their bodily movements and our own as the specific sorts of actions they are.

But proceed in the reverse direction. Regard what happens when a person performs an action in total abstraction from any of the background circumstances that operate in our normal understanding of actions and agents. It is not a motorist, employer, employee, a member of some family and so on upon whom we gaze. All reasons are ruled out of order in the account of what is taking place which might carry our thoughts to matters of policy, rules, statutes, maxims or principles, or to any circumstances which inject even a tacit reference to the transactions in which we engage with others, *e.g.* to things one might do if ordered to do so, asked to do so and so on. Not even a 'No reason' will be admitted as a relevant answer to the question 'Why?' Regarded in this way, what one would see is no longer a person or an action, but something which if it irritates one might brush aside in just the sort of way in which one straightens out an annoying wrinkle in the rug on the floor. No wonder we are disturbed by the shooting incident described by Camus in *The Stranger*; here we are invited to share the shocking experience of seeing bodily movements and bodies in this totally dehumanized way—and the *experience* is almost too much for us, for it requires a *total* estrangement from others.[1] And it is an experience, not an interpretation which we place on what we

[1] I owe the recognition of the relevance of this example to Professor Herbert Morris.

see, when unlike Camus' stranger we see as we normally do the actions of human beings.

But how does all of this explain the concepts of agent and action? Can it be enough to call attention to the difference between these experiences—the experience of one who sees a given bodily movement as the action of a person and one who views it in the disturbing, even shocking, manner of Camus' character (or, to take another case, one who sees it perhaps as tissue, muscles and bones in motion as a physiologist does)? And granted that training, including the training in the use of discourse itself, is essential to our understanding of bodily movements as actions, how does this enable us to understand what actions and agents are? Must we not in effect concede the point of the objection that in taking for our starting point the notion of an agent acting for a reason in a given human situation, we are abandoning any attempt to explain what an action and what an agent *really* are?

This dissatisfaction arises from the fact that one wants to know what an action as such is (never mind the conceptual connection between actions, agents, desires, intentions, etc., or the character of the discourse applicable to actions as distinct from bodily movements, or the character of the very lives and experiences in which those bodily movements may be treated as actions)—whatever else may be said, what is it *just* to act? And so, too, with agent—granted that an agent is such-and-such a person, a motorist, mother, teacher, student, etc., etc., granted, too, that the distinctive character of the lives, actions, experiences and discourse are describable in such-and-such a way—what one wants to know is just what it is to be an agent, a being who acts, and never mind anything *further* that may be said.

But suppose someone asked 'What is it to be a chesspiece, and what is it to be a chess-player?', how shall one explain? Would we not have to call attention to the fact that there are various sorts of chess-pieces, each with its characteristic moves, that these are made on a board of play, that the game starts with a certain arrangement of pieces on the board, that certain forms of discourse are employed during the course of play (*e.g.* 'Check!') and that a certain eventuality constitutes winning the game? Would we not have to explain the game so that our inquirer could have some understanding of the moves made by chess-players? And if he insisted that all of this was beside the point, that what he wanted to know was not how this or that chess-move was made, but what it is to be a chess-move and a chess-player *as such*—never mind the connections of such concepts with those of winning or losing, the descriptions of the moves that could be given in terms of the intentions of the players in carrying out tactical or strategic plans, the forms of discourse that operate in the conduct of the play or even the skills and intelligence exhibited in the play which are developed by training and study—what *could* we understand him to be asking for? Is it that he is a strange being who is totally unfamiliar with playing for the amusement it provides; or, less unfortunately, with games conducted in accordance with rules? But then in neither case will he have understood the explanation he has asked for, and the remedy is to try to make him understand by getting him to play a game according to rules. And if the complaint

194

is that this background familiarity is taken for granted in the explanation given, then the reply surely is that any explanation starts from some initial basis of understanding and unless *this* basis of understanding is present, neither the question nor the answer will be intelligible. This indeed is the stultifying character of this demand for an account of a chess-move *as such*: the demand that we ignore precisely what is crucial to an understanding of any explanation that can be given—the characteristically and distinctively human phenomenon of playing a game according to rules which training and training alone can make intelligible, training without which no discourse about games, questions or answers can be understood. For a being without the experience of playing games and doing things according to rules, no explanation of these human activities will serve to render them intelligible; every account of their actions will invite an insatiable 'Why?' and nothing in principle will serve to render intelligible the familiar discourse we understand.

So it is in the case of actions and agents. Here the training received by the very young child in responding to those about it plays a decisive rôle in the ability it acquires, not only to recognize the bodily movements of those with whom it has dealings as the actions they are, but also to recognize others as agents and in so doing to grasp the familiar concepts of action and agent. There is no such thing as the concept of an action or an agent *as such*. To act is to perform this or that particular action in this or that particular situation. Let it be granted that an adult may do something for no reason at all. But it is logically impossible

195

that this should be the universal rule. And let it be granted that an agent may do something that does not involve any traffic with any others, for a man or indeed a child may brush off an annoying fly. Here, again, it is logically impossible that this should be the universal rule. For our concept of an action is the concept of an action for which the agent may have a reason and a reason of the kind that relates to the social intercourse of agents. What is central, therefore, to the very young child's understanding of the concepts of agents and actions is the recognition which it acquires, *through training*, of its and others' actions in the familiar transactions in which it engages with them. For if it is to distinguish between objects and persons and hence between happenings—agreeable or disagreeable as these may be—and the actions of persons, it must acquire a recognition, not of persons and actions as such, but of *this* or *that* particular person and of *this* or *that* particular action of some specific person with which it deals. It must recognize that it is being commanded, comforted, fed, asked, played with, taught, succoured, questioned, clothed, etc., etc. (and of its rôle in these matters), by those whose status within the family are defined by the manner in which they carry on these proceedings with it. Here, training plays an essential rôle, including the training involved in the use of discourse, in the acquisition by the child of the abilities, skills and intelligence involved in these transactions. But it is just in the context of these homely activities that the child recognizes the persons with whom it deals as specific persons— as mother or father. For the child's concept of a mother is not that of the physiologist's or geneticist's but rather that of a person upon whom it is dependent in distinctive and peculiarly important ways. So too with that of a father.[1]

But this is only the beginning. For the concepts of person and action which we have are concepts enriched by the whole character of our discourse about such matters, not only by the logical connections of these with other concepts but by the possible descriptions applicable to persons and their actions. For an understanding of this body of discourse, training again is essential—the training the child receives as it comes to be guided by a complex network of social and moral conventions, principles, rules, maxims and policies in its conduct and in its relations with others. It is not enough to point to the distinctive character of the discourse we apply to persons and agents; what needs to be emphasized in what lies so close to us that it escapes our notice: such discourse is no mere string of words and sentences uttered by contemplative beings but forms of communication employed by beings in their day-to-day transactions with one another. It is in these transactions in which, by the training and the instruction we have received, we have come to participate with others, that the explanation of the concepts of person and agent come ultimately to rest.

Still, it may be argued that, all training apart, this account is premised upon our understanding of what it is for a very young child to act, and hence that the explanation of the concept of action is circular. But our account of action involves a good deal more than

[1] Cf. my discussion of the concept of a father in *Rights and Right Conduct*.

can possibly be ascribed to the child, and all of this has been described at least in general terms. Still, the child does act, and how shall one explain the concept of an action, truncated as it may be, when applied to the infant? But even here there has been no resort to indefinables. At least *some* of the features of the concepts of action and person we apply to adults are present here, *e.g.* the logical connections of this concept with that of desire, reasons for doing, experience, etc., albeit in a restricted or limited way. Our explanation must come to rest somewhere and at least at this point that in the case of an infant we have a human being, undeveloped and rudimentary as it may be. In what sense are we to explain *this* fact? How except in human terms can a human being be understood?— Still, a child acts and so does an adult, so there must be something in common; and what they have in common is, surely, that both act, both are persons. But this is to look for the characteristics of an action and of a person as such. One can *say* that one wants to know what these are, but one can also bark at the moon.

CHAPTER FOURTEEN

CONCLUSION—DECISION, CHOICE, PREDICTION AND THE VOLUNTARY

IN Chapter II, I discussed very briefly the question whether or not explanations of action in terms of the character of the agent are causal explanations and in particular whether or not actions that are out of character can be explained in terms of interfering causal factors. It will be remembered that I quickly turned the discussion to an inquiry into the nature of the actions which such allegedly causal accounts are designed to explain. In the argument just concluded I have attempted to show that it is a fundamental mistake to suppose that the causal model employed in the natural sciences will fit the everyday explanations of actions in terms of intentions, interests, desires, etc. It is not even our concern, in asking *how* someone did such-and-such, to inquire into the natural history of his action, to probe, as it were, behind the scene of human action itself, to discover events in an area that constitutes the general causal condition of action. For the answer to the question 'How did . . .?', does not remove us from the scene of human conduct; it specifies, rather, an *action* in the performance of which the agent was able to do what he did. Indeed, the action specified in the answer may even be the very same action as the one explained. Thus if I am asked how I signalled (or how I got into the house without a key), the reply that I did so by raising my arm (or by climbing through the window) refers the questioner to an action which in the given circumstances is the very same action as the one for which an explanation was sought. In any case, whether the question is 'Why?' or 'How?', the concern is not with logically self-contained events which stand in some empirically discovered causal relation to one another, but with human events. It is hardly necessary at this point to inquire into the logical features of our descriptions of the character of persons. Their logical connection with action, the interests, desires, motives, habits, etc., of agents is surely evident. It follows that there is a radical disparity between these two modes of explanation: causal explanations of events and our familiar explanations of human actions.

It is this radical disparity that accounts for the characteristic ambivalences and contradictions in current psychological discussions. Insofar as psychologists are obsessed with the desire to establish their inquiry on a parallel footing with the natural sciences, the search is on for mechanisms in terms of which explanations of conduct are to be given. Conduct viewed in this way becomes 'overt behaviour', an ambiguous term that effectively obscures the all-important distinction between bodily movements or happenings and actions. As bodily movements, items of overt behaviour are physiological occurrences for which physiological occurrences would appear to be sufficient causal conditions. In that case psychology reduces to physiology, and the alleged explanations of human action have succeeded only in changing the subject, in substituting explanations of bodily movements for explanations of action. For absolutely nothing about any matter of human conduct follows logically from any account of the physiological conditions of bodily movement. If this gap between matters of physiological fact and matters of human action is to be bridged, at least some token concessions must be made to our everyday discourse about persons and their actions. Some mental terms must be retained in the speculations about the mechanism of human conduct. Not infrequently, however, and precisely in order to maintain the fiction of the application of the causal model, homely terms like 'desire', 'person', etc., are eschewed and instead the talk is about 'organism', 'drive', etc. And, not unexpectedly, fatal stresses and strains appear in the uses to which this jargon is put. The word 'drive' is a notorious example: as an interior movement—some sort of causal factor—a drive is blind, fully intelligible without reference to anything to which it might give rise; as something telic it is logically essential that it refer us to that to which the agent is driven—his action.

Does the rejection of the causal model imply that actions are uncaused, that freedom is to be purchased at the expense of a capricious indeterminism, or of a libertarianism that misrepresents every responsible action as an heroic effort that somehow thwarts the causal order? Quite the contrary, the argument is designed to show the logical incoherence involved in the supposition that actions, desires, intentions, etc., stand in causal relations, either in the Humean sense or in any sense in which the term 'causal' is employed in the natural sciences. And if the argument is correct, determinism, if it employs this sense of cause, is not false but radically confused. So it is with indeterminism and libertarianism which grant to determinism the intelligibility of employing the causal model— these seek to avoid the conclusion that each of us is the hapless victim of events, in the former case by viewing actions as causally indeterminate happenings, in the latter by viewing actions for which a person is responsible as events produced by extraordinary and mysterious self-exertions. The trouble in all these cases is that the applicability in principle of the causal model is taken for granted. Given this fatal blunder, actions degenerate into mere bodily happenings, produced or not as each of these doctrines would have it; and once this conceptual mistake has been made the way is open to a radical misunderstanding of desires, intentions, decisions, etc., as internal events that can operate in some sort of mechanism of the mind.

Notorious in this connection is the all too frequent talk about the causality of decision and choice, as if a decision or choice were some sort of inner 'oomph' that sparked something (but what?—an action, or a bodily movement?) into being. Surely it would be absurd to attempt to make out the distinction between bodily movement and action by reference to either decision or choice. For it is not true that agents decide or choose to do everything they do. If, for example, I go to the corner grocer to purchase a dozen eggs, it may well be that I have decided to do just that. But do I, when I pick up each egg and place it in a bag, then go on to make one decision or twelve—one for each egg? And if I pick up two eggs at a time, do I make one or two decisions? Must I, once I have decided to go to the grocer to purchase eggs, make any further decisions in the matter? Often, at least, I simply go to the grocer, and as a matter of course without giving the matter any further thought, pick up the eggs I see and put them in a bag. And if, say, I scratch my head or blow my nose, do I *decide* to do such things? So with choosing—must I choose to do everything I do? Perhaps I choose to purchase eggs rather than meat. But must I choose this egg rather than that egg when I pick up the former and not the latter? I might if I were selecting eggs for size; but often at least I do nothing of the sort—I just pick up each egg as it comes to hand. If I give my wallet to someone who holds a pistol to my head, *must* I have decided to do so, chosen to do so? It would be *a priorism* at its worst to say that, even when I am terrified—as indeed I would be in such a case—and act as I do, there must have been choice or decision. And, finally, deciding cannot possibly be an interior Humean cause of doing (and so too with choosing) for reasons that parallel precisely those given for the case of desire. If I decide to do X, the decision is intelligible only as the decision *to do X*. The reference to the doing is logically essential to the very thought of the decision. So too with choice, when in choosing between objects A and B, I choose to take A. Far from carrying us behind the scenes of action to events that somehow produce action, decisions and choices are intelligible only within the arena of action. By reference to them we may characterize, not bodily movements as actions (for that they are actions we already know when we ask whether a person has decided or chosen to act as he does), but actions as those the agent has decided or chosen to do and hence actions for which reasons of one sort or another can be given. It is, therefore, essential to decision and choice—no mere logical accident as it were—that there be agents, actions and reasons for doing.

Granted all this, do we not speak of the causes of a person's action? Do we not predict what persons will do, and if one can predict precisely and exactly what a person will do, must there not be causes of his doing which would justify such predictions? Again, some actions are voluntary, others involuntary; we say, as circumstances warrant, that a person could or could not have done otherwise; we recognize that some have and others do not have much will-power; and that some acts are and others are not performed of the agent's own free will. How can we avoid the irresistible conclusion that in various ways causal conditions of doings are applicable to human conduct?

It is certainly true that we use 'cause' in speaking about the actions of agents, but we can no more infer from this verbal consideration that actions are the Humean effects of events than we can from the etymological derivation of the term 'motive'. Earlier I discussed the impropriety in general of supposing that a motive is a Humean cause, but I examined in detail only the case of intention. 'Motive' covers a variety of items, not only the intention a person may have in doing something but also such items as anger, jealousy, revenge, etc. Consider the most likely candidate for Humean cause: the sudden flare-up of anger that causes a man to spank his child. Even here the Humean model will not fit in the way in which it fits the case of a blow on the patella which causes a man's leg to jerk up. In the latter case the person, his thoughts, his concerns, his intentions, reasons, etc., are wholly irrelevant to the occurrence thus produced. It is not that the blow causes *him* to jerk his leg, but rather that the blow caused, not something the man did, but a happening, the jerking of the leg. In the case of the angry man, the anger caused *the man* to act as he does. Anger indeed is no mere Humean impression of reflection; for it is logically essential to the concept of anger that the anger be about or over something. It is no more possible for a person to be angry about nothing than for a person to have a desire that is not a desire for something. And even here it is not causal knowledge that enables a man to say that he spanked his child because he was angry as it is in the case of one who explains the movement of the leg by a 'Because it was struck in the patellar region'. It is rather that the reference to his anger explains the action as that of an angry man—it enables us to describe *what* he did. And this by no means ends the matter, for anger may be justified or unjustified and the person in giving way to it may be blameable on account of it. Nothing of this sort applies to the jerk of the leg that results from the blow on the patella. Here we do not have an action of an agent but the action of the leg, namely, a bodily movement.

'Cause', then, is one of the snare words in both ordinary and philosophical speech, and here every attention to the precise manner in which it is employed is essential. For even in cases in which we have an immediate response (*e.g.* the startled jump of a person when a fire-cracker suddenly explodes behind him, or the scream of terror at the sight of the apparition on the stairs, or the sudden withdrawal of the hand from the hot object one has touched), in which there is neither calculation nor any of the other evidences of reasoned or intentional conduct, the question is not 'What caused the action?' but 'What caused him (or her) to do . . . (to jump, scream, or withdraw the hand)?' Here the reference to the agent is essential in the way in which it is not in the case of the reflex jerk of the leg, the twitch of a muscle or the movement of the intestines. And here we have extreme cases which shade almost imperceptibly (when we consider the broad and varied spectrum of cases to which the question 'What caused him (or her) to . . .?' is applicable) into the cases in which there is calculated and reasoned behaviour, in which the agent is getting what he wants for good and sufficient reasons. The important thing is not to be blinded by the fact that 'cause' may be used in all cases but to recognize just how it is applied and in what varied ways to cases that range from instinctive responses to reasoned, rational transactions of agents with one another. In none of these cases, varied though they may be, is causation in the sense in which this term applies to physical events applicable to the actions of agents. But a detailed inquiry into these uses of 'cause' is not possible within the limits of this essay.

Equally treacherous is the term 'prediction'. Granted that to predict is to say what will be the case, what does *this* mean? I can be said to say what will be by promising that I shall do such-and-such. By declaring that I shall hit the target, I can be said to say what will be, and then proving it by exhibiting my skill. I can be said to say what will be by contradicting someone's expression of intention, *e.g.* 'I won't let you harm that child!' and succeeding. I can be said to say what will be by saying that the coin will fall heads and having my guess come true. I can be said to say what will be by predicting the villainous act of someone I know to be a villain. I can be said to say what will be by predicting the path of a comet from its known velocity, direction of motion, etc. And so on. Here someone may object that after all there must be something common to all of these cases— saying what will be—whatever the differences between them might be. Certainly, in all of these and other cases of prediction this is common: something is said about the future. But to say this is only to say that these words apply. It is not to say that there is a common ingredient so that promising, for example, is saying what will be plus something else that makes the saying a promise and not, say, an expression of my resolution. What makes the promise a promise is not that there is one item—saying what will be— together with some other item. It is, rather, as I have argued elsewhere, that the saying what will be when it is done by an agent under such-and-such circumstances (and here it is no matter what goes on in the mind of the person speaking) is the very same thing as, and not part of, promising.[1] The formula 'saying what will be' is singularly unhelpful. It would be just as unilluminating to say that in all cases in which we use the term 'cause', whether in speaking about the causes of the contractions of muscles or in speaking

[1] Cf. 'On Promising', *Mind*, January 1956.

about the actions of agents (what caused him to do), there is something common to which we are referring —but of what and in what sense of 'cause' is the crucially important question. And if I predict that someone I know and fully understand—for I know the kind of person he is, the sorts of character traits he has, the things he wants and the goods with which he is concerned—will in such-and-such circumstances act in such-and-such a way, this is not at all like predicting the path of a satellite; nor does the reliability of my prediction rest upon hidden causal factors that operate in such a way as to make true what I say will be the case. For here the reliability of my prediction rests upon my understanding of the person —he is like an open book to me—not upon hidden Humean causal factors about which, if they were at all relevant, I can at best only speculate. Here nothing is hidden; it is because I understand him, not because I am aware of events transpiring in some alleged mechanism of his mind or body, that I am able to say what he will do.

Such predictions sometimes go wrong. Suppose, however, it were possible in principle to predict with perfect accuracy, how could one then maintain that the agent could do anything other than what he does, that his behaviour is not subject to causal factors in precisely the way in which this is admittedly true of the motions of some heavenly body, that a human being is not a helpless victim of circumstances within and without him? Here we have the picture of a human being reacting to stimuli from without in accordance with the precise character of his constitution—the pattern of events within his nervous system

—an extraordinarily complex mechanical or electronic system no different in principle, but only in degree of complexity, from some of the self-regulating mechanisms of the laboratory which perform their perfectly predictable operations when suitably programmed.

This picture wholly misrepresents the character of agents and their actions. What would one predict—actions or bodily movements? Certainly, if one knew the state of the nervous system and musculature, then one could predict, given such-and-such stimulation, that, say, the arm would rise in the air. But our concern is not with the rising of the arm but with the person's raising of his arm; and with raising his arm, say, in order to signal, to get what he wants, and so on. Let it be that the nervous system of one who has been trained to drive and to give the signal that he is about to make a turn has been suitably 'conditioned'—that there are characteristic brain patterns present in these and only these cases at the time the arm is raised in order to give the signal—further conditions are required for the raising of the arm, and what can these be? It is no good saying that these conditions are the appropriate visual and auditory stimuli, the nervous excitation of the end-organs in the eye or ear. For so far all that such stimulations of the appropriately conditioned bodily mechanism can produce is the movement of the arm. In order that one might predict that the person will raise his arm in order to give the signal, one needs not only a knowledge of the central nervous system and of the appropriate stimulation of the end-organs, but also of the circumstances in which the *agent*—not the bodily mechanism—is placed and of what, in these circumstances, he will do. We

need to know, in short, that we have an agent, a motorist, who is driving and whose action of raising the arm
is to be understood in terms of the appropriate rule
of the road as a case of signalling a turn as the cross-
road comes into view. But in that case we have left
behind all reference to hypothetical occurrences in the
nervous system, for now we are back to the scene of
human action. And the circumstances to which we
must now attend, if we are to predict that he will raise
his arm to signal, are not Humean causal conditions
of his doing. They are rather circumstances in the
context of which the bodily movement that does occur,
and however it may be that it is produced, *is* understood as the specific action it is.

'Condition' is in fact the source of a great deal of
confusion in the philosophical literature. Sometimes
it refers to a legal requirement or stipulation; sometimes to an event related to that of which it is a condition by some fact of causation or by some law of
nature; sometimes to an action (*e.g.* as in 'I shall do
such-and-such on condition that you do . . .'); sometimes to the circumstance in which a matter of fact
is also a reason for doing (*e.g.* my wanting food is the
condition in which 'There is a restaurant across the
street' is a reason for my going there), and so on. In
the present case, the conditions or circumstances in
which the bodily movement occurs—an agent who is
a motorist and who is executing his intention, guided
by the rules of the road and a variety of considerations
as the turn in the road approaches—*constitute* or
define the bodily movement as the action it is.

Here someone may object: granted that there is no
one central nuclear experience that constitutes the

intention of an agent, and similarly in the case of a
desire or a decision or a choice, still these do make a
difference to the character of a man's thoughts and
feelings, *i.e.* to his inner mental state. And if so, there
must be corresponding sorts of neural events, however
complex these may be, in each of these cases. So too
with the circumstances in which a motorist finds himself and to which he attends as he performs his various
actions. If he attends to these, if he has been trained,
if he executes his skilful performances, there are
characteristic states of the nervous system and
characteristic exciting stimuli. Now if one knew enough
about the nervous system, could we not 'interpret' or
'decode' such states and stimuli as the states and
stimuli of such-and-such an agent doing such-and-
such in the given sort of circumstances? And given a
knowledge of the future stimuli, similarly 'decoded',
could we not infallibly predict such-and-such bodily
movements, similarly decipherable as the bodily
movements performed by the given sort of agent in
doing such-and-such? No doubt such predictability
would depend on our own status as agents who can
understand cases of bodily movements as cases of
actions and who can recognize that in given circumstances the actions in question would be of a given
sort; but we could, given this understanding that
would enable us to interpret neural data in the appropriate way, predict on the basis of such data what any
given person will do. If so, could we still insist that
any agent, even when he attends carefully to what he is
doing, even when his behaviour is as calculated and as
deliberate as it may be, could possibly have done
otherwise? And since he in turn, equipped with the

same ability, could discover, predict and interpret the neural data in *our* nervous systems, are we not equally helpless in all that we do—even in discussing these very matters? And if so, we seem to be on the brink of insanity—it is as if computing machines were to be programmed and decoded only by other machines of like sorts, as if work were being done in a laboratory without any person doing it.

What we know about the nervous system and the events transpiring in it as we think, feel and do is extraordinarily little, but the reply need not rest on such an appeal to our manifest ignorance. Indeed, one should hope and pray that it may be possible one day to know enough about the mechanism of the body to enable qualified persons to cure mental disorders by introducing the necessary changes in the central nervous system, perhaps by means of surgery. One may grant, in fact, that the development of the central nervous system goes hand-in-hand with the maturation of human beings as they acquire the varied skills which they exhibit in their reasoned and responsible thoughts and actions, that the latter is in some way dependent upon the former. But none of this implies the forbidding picture painted by the epiphenomenalist in which the status of a person reduces to the vaporous after-effects of physiological processes. For even if we could do the decoding, we should still have the central nervous system of a person who reasons, justifies, decides, chooses, intends, wants, and conducts himself as he does with other persons about him. Indeed, what our speculation implies is the requirement, for the thoughts and actions of such persons, of requisite states of the nervous system and this, far from reducing persons to hapless mechanisms, is only a more radical representation of the familiar view that persons are not disembodied spirits but persons who can be seen and touched and hurt, who use their arms, legs, etc. in the actions they perform, and who require for such employment of their limbs and other bodily parts certain general conditions and particular states of their nervous systems. Indeed, the alleged conclusion that each of us is a helpless victim of the events transpiring in the central nervous system is simply a logical howler. 'Could have done' and 'could not have done', 'helpless', etc.—these are expressions employed not with respect to events occurring in the mechanism of the body, nor to mental events, whether or not these are regarded as mere by-products of bodily processes—Humean effects of neural events—but to *persons*. We do not say that an itch or twitch, a feeling, thought or desire, however we understand these, is helpless. Neither do we say that the body is helpless in any sense in which we say this about a person. It is *persons* who are able or unable to do or to refrain from doing; to think or to refrain from thinking, etc. We need, in short, to recognize the necessary starting point for any elucidation of expressions of these sorts —persons who act, think, feel, in their commerce with the things about them and with each other. This is the language-game in which expressions like 'could have done', 'could not have done', 'helpless', etc., are employed, in any sense in which they bear upon questions of the freedom of human action. To suppose that they can be employed, without radical distortion or change, in the account of the events within the body, or in any account of their Humean effects, is the confusion upon which the apparently disastrous consequences of our speculative assumption rests.

But still, if our speculation about the decoding were granted, would it not be possible, not merely to predict how human beings would behave, but also and without their knowledge to control them by altering the neural conditions within their bodies? Certainly. In point of fact, other devices are currently employed by politicians and others concerned to manipulate human beings—the difference is only one of degree in the success of the results; the methods currently employed are fortunately very crude and frequently inefficacious. And if by introducing an electrode into the brain of a person, I succeed in getting him to believe that he is Napoleon, that surely is not a rational belief that he has, nor is he responsible for what he does in consequence of this belief, however convinced he may be that he is fully justified in acting as he does. There would be no virtue in any philosophical doctrine which ruled out the possibility that human beings may be controlled, that by virtue of what we do to them we may render them incompetent, insane, devoid of responsibility. But here as before, we can understand terms like 'competence', 'control', 'responsible' only by keeping clearly in mind the contexts appropriate to their employment—human beings who are rational in and attentive to what they are doing in their transactions with one another and in their dealings with the things about them.

In short, even on our speculative assumption, nothing disastrous to our common beliefs about the freedom of human action would follow. Such knowledge might be dangerous—it might open the way to abuses in the management of human beings. But even if this knowledge were achieved, we should still employ our familiar discourse in describing persons and their conduct. Far from it being the case that the possibility of such knowledge implies the helplessness of human beings in all of their thoughts and actions, the achievement of such knowledge would enable us to understand, in a two-fold sense, why human beings think, desire, choose, decide and do as in fact they do. For one thing, we should have a knowledge of the neural conditions under which such human events occur; and, for another, since the neural states and events would be 'decoded', these would be understood in terms that go beyond the purview of the physiologist. In effect, then, the knowledge of such decoded neural states and events would indeed give us a fuller understanding of the actions of responsible persons and hence a better basis for prediction than we now have; but it would do this *only* by revealing more fully their characters, interests, desires, hopes, social and moral rôles, choices, intentions, etc.—just those sorts of items in terms of which we do in fact explain and predict the actions of human beings. We should then be able, for one thing, to understand, explain and predict the quite rational, responsible actions of free agents; and we should then be able to understand and to predict that such agents would decide not to perform actions of various sorts, in circumstances to which they were attending, and which they could then and there have done, for this or that reason.

What needs to be emphasized again and again is

the fact that there *are* contexts appropriate to the use of expressions like 'could have done' and 'could not have done'. In his justly celebrated 'Ifs and Cans', **J. L. Austin** has exposed some of the confusions that surround these and other locutions—confusions that are the immediate consequence of the failure to recognize the relevant details of the circumstances in which such locutions are familiarly employed.[1] Here I can only repeat that these locutions are intelligibly employed only in the context of human action—this, not events in the nervous system or bodily movements in which these issue, is the language-game in which they are intelligibly employed.

But what of the distinction between the voluntary and the involuntary? Surely this is one of the most central matters that requires comment and explanation even in a preliminary study, such as this one, of matters that are basic to the concept of a free and responsible action—one of the very first items on the agenda of any discussion of this concept! I want to say, on the contrary, that it must be one of the *last*, important as the distinction between the voluntary and the involuntary in fact is. Here indeed is one of the most gravely misunderstood pairs of terms in the philosophical vocabulary.

The familiar view is that the distinction is to be made in terms of the order of the causes of action: a voluntary action is one that is somehow produced by the will—acts of volition; an involuntary action is one that proceeds from other events. So prevalent and

[1] The Annual Philosophical Lecture, Henriette Herz Trust, *Proceedings of the British Academy*, Vol. XLII, London: Oxford University Press.

insistent has this view been that it has seeped into some dictionary accounts of these terms. But if by 'will' is intended the causal agency that consists in the occurrence of such acts of volition, then there is no will and, as I argued earlier in Chapter V, there cannot possibly be any since the conception of acts of volition or willings, by means of which actions allegedly are performed, is self-contradictory. Yet 'will' can be used quite unobjectionably; for we do speak of a person's will in such-and-such a matter, of a person of good will, of a person with a will of iron, of persons who do or refrain from doing of their own free will, and so on. So, too, with the term 'volition'—this does not refer us to interior acts of volition hidden in the recesses of the mind which are the alleged effective agents in the production of actions, but to perfectly familiar items in the lives of human beings. A man's will in such-and-such a matter may be simply what he wants or wishes. A person of good will is one who is a morally estimable agent who is concerned in his thought and action with the well-being of others no less than with his obligations towards them. A man with a will of iron is one who is unusually steadfast in executing his intentions, undeterred by considerations that would distract or prevent most people from achieving their goals. And if we are to understand what is involved in the idea of someone doing something of his own free will we must look to the centrally important and fully enriched cases in which a rational, indeed a moral, agent chooses and decides to act as he does for reasons he considers good and proper. This is not to say that every action done of one's own free will is one chosen or decided; or that every such action is one performed for a moral reason. It is rather that 'free will' is not ascribed to any agent other than a moral agent capable of rational choice and decision. Just as it is logically impossible for someone always to want something for no reason whatsoever, so it is logically impossible for someone always to act of his own free will without rational and moral choice and decision. It is only by reference to such cases of persons who act as they do on the basis of the rational, and indeed moral, choices and decisions they make for reasons they consider good and sufficient that the conception of free will can be fully elucidated.

Once we recognize the diversity of items that come under the term 'will'—reasons, desires, decisions, choices, intentions, etc., each of which in the requisite sense explains an agent's conduct—it is possible to understand some of the otherwise perplexing features of some of the uses of 'voluntary' and 'involuntary'. For one thing, these are by no means exhaustive terms; that is to say, it is not every action that is either voluntary or involuntary. If, for example, I rub my nose, this is not something I need do because I have any intention in doing it, or a desire to do so; nor need I decide or choose to do so. I simply do it—period. Hence with respect to this action, the answer to the question 'Voluntary or involuntary?' is correctly given by saying 'Neither, don't be absurd!' And the absurdity of asking 'Which is it?' is by no means due to the fact that the terms 'voluntary' and 'involuntary' apply, as some have suggested, only to actions that are objectionable, untoward or unusual. It is rather that in this case it is manifest that I have no intention, desire or reason for doing it that might serve to reveal its import in any transaction in which I engage—none of the items covered by the term 'the will' serves to explain it. I simply do, and that is all. In the second place, the terms 'voluntary' and 'involuntary' are not even mutually exclusive. Suppose, for example, a young man has committed some crime, which so far has not been charged to him. But instead of waiting to be discovered, tracked down and arrested, he goes to the police and gives himself up. Certainly the police would consider this action to be voluntary— he gives himself up not because he is ordered to do so by an arresting officer, but for reasons which have nothing to do with any of the functions of the police. But suppose, further, that our youth does this, not by choice but under the threat of his father to disinherit him if he does not do so, and let us suppose, further, that the crime is a minor one which nonetheless carries with it a disagreeable punishment. In this case, he gives himself up against his will and only in order to avoid the far more disagreeable prospect of disinheritance. Surely we would distinguish this involuntary action from the voluntary action of one who, having committed a crime, gives himself up because he has chosen to submit to the punishment which he recognizes he deserves.

Now there is no difficulty in understanding how the same action—appearing at the police station to give oneself up—can be characterized in these two distinct ways: as voluntary by the arresting police officer, as involuntary both by the agent and by those aware of the further circumstances with which the police officer is unacquainted. For the action of giving oneself up is, in these further circumstances, the further action of submitting to the pressure exerted by the father. There is no difficulty, then, in seeing how it is that the same action—walking into the police station and announcing that one has committed such-and-such a crime—may be characterized as voluntary when understood in one way and as involuntary when understood in quite a different way. Here everything depends upon *what* the action of walking into the police station is; and what it is is determined by his intention in doing this, his reasons, his desires, in short, just those items that come under the general heading of the term 'will'.

But how does this establish that the terms 'voluntary' and 'involuntary' are not mutually exclusive? All that has been shown is that the action of walking into the police station can be understood further in two quite different ways—in the one case as the action of submitting to the authority of the police, in the other as submitting to the threat of one's father—as two quite distinct actions. But given that the action of giving oneself up has been *properly* understood, is it not then settled which of the two—voluntary or involuntary—it must be?

Here, however, we need to recognize the import of the terms 'voluntary' and 'involuntary' and the ways in which these reflect our interests in conduct. As moral agents surveying the scene, our concern may well be with the moral character of the young man and his conduct. Given this interest, we do need to know whether he wanted to do the legally and morally required thing and hence whether, in giving himself up in order to accept the legal consequences of his crime, he was doing this in order to save his precious inheritance or in order to receive his just deserts. To ask whether an action is voluntary is, in effect, to ask whether further questions about his intentions, his desires, his reasons, are relevant. But such a question is never asked out of the blue, but only in a context in which the questioner has a quite particular interest in the action. And since, as moral agents, our interest in an action is the interest we have in affixing the measures of praise or blame appropriate to it, we do need to know something more about the agent's further intentions, his further reasons, etc., than appear on the surface and which enable us to understand the moral features of what the person has done. But our interests are not always moral. A policeman's concern with the action of one who has committed a crime may be quite circumscribed by the legal responsibility, determined by the character of his office, which he has in dealing with him. It is quite irrelevant to his legal office that our young man has been led to come into the police station for this or that morally commendable reason. All that he need be concerned with is the fact that our young man has submitted to the authority of the police without having set into motion by his crime the usual operations of the police in tracking him down and compelling him to surrender. From this point of view, giving himself up as he has is submitting himself to the authority of the police. Whether or not he wants to do this because it is right or because he wants to save his inheritance is of no matter to the policeman's interest in the affair insofar as it is determined by his office; the action of giving himself up, which our young man does for whatever reason he may have, is from the point of view of the policeman's interest in the action voluntary. It may be that the policeman in seeing the young man give himself up has not *fully* understood the action, that failing to appreciate that he is doing it in order to avoid disinheritance he fails to recognize that he is submitting to the pressures of his father and that he is in this way providing for his own future; nonetheless he has most certainly *properly* understood it. For this is not at all like the case of a criminal who absent-mindedly or inadvertently walks into a police station while on his way to cash a check—here one would have neither a full nor a proper understanding if one supposed that he was giving himself up even if it led to his being marched into a cell. In our example, giving oneself up *is* submitting to the authority of the police and *this* action, so described, can be characterized either as voluntary or as involuntary, depending upon one's interest in the action and hence upon what knowledge of the agent's interests, desires, reasons, etc., is relevant to one's proper understanding of the action. The fact that the same action, properly understood, may be correctly characterized as either voluntary or involuntary depends upon the fact that different features of the agent's will may or may not be relevant to the different interests a person may have in the action.

Generally, it is impossible, in the abstract and without reference to those features of an action that reflect the quite particular interests one may have in it, to answer the question 'Voluntary or involuntary?' This question is never asked out of the blue, as it were, but only within the context of some interest we have in appraising the action. There are limiting cases, of course. We do speak of the voluntary and the involuntary movements of parts of the body (for example, of the arm and of the heart respectively), but only because such movements can occur in actions performed by the agent which may be of any interest to him or to anyone else in the ordinary circumstances of human events. The centrally important uses of 'voluntary' and 'involuntary' are those which refer us to the scene of social and moral conduct, where actions performed by one agent have a bearing upon the lives and actions of others. And where diverse and even conflicting interests are involved, it is not surprising that the very same action should be characterized as voluntary by one person, as involuntary by another. Consider how complex are the issues involved in deciding whether the action of a soldier is voluntary or involuntary when, for example, it takes the form of obeying the order of one's commanding officer to shoot at random one dozen inhabitants of a hostile village, and where it is done without hesitation and even with satisfaction! A great deal hinges upon whether we decide the action to be voluntary. Shall we be led in our judgment to consider only the military propriety, perhaps necessity, of obeying one's commanding officer? If our interest is moral, shall we say that his brutish satisfaction marks the voluntary character of the action, that it cannot be involuntary since that would serve to absolve the soldier of all moral responsibility? Shall we say that the soldier's action is voluntary whether or not he derived satisfaction from it? Can we demand of a soldier that he risk court martial and even death by refusing to obey an order? Here the issues become exceedingly complex—our judgment that the action is voluntary or involuntary as the case may be is bound up with important and difficult issues that reflect not only diverse and even divergent interests but difficult matters of moral principles, legal rules, political and social policies.

INDEX

225